Juss
Microwaving

by Ruby Schile Juss

Juss Microwaving
by Ruby Schile Juss

Juss Microwaving Publishing Co.
P.O. Box 762
Medicine Hat, Alberta
Canada T1A 7G7

First Edition October 1983
Second Edition June 1984

Canadian Cataloguing in Publication Data

Juss, Ruby Schile, 1943-
Juss microwaving

Includes index.
ISBN 0-9691453-1-4

1. Microwave cookery. I. Title.
TX832.J87 1983   641.5'882   C83-091352-1

Production, Design and Editing by
Cover to Cover Inc.
Regina, Saskatchewan, Canada

Printed in Canada by
D. W. Friesen and Sons, Ltd., Altona, Manitoba

Introduction

Ruby Schile Juss has been teaching cooking classes for five years at the Medicine Hat College as well as the surrounding community. She has done demonstrations on microwave cooking in schools, department stores and churches as well as teaching her own family to use a microwave.

Microwave cooking has become a safe, nutritious and quick way to prepare food. The use of microwaves has become widely spread throughout North America to include restaurants, offices and hospitals as well as a majority of homes. They are easily transported, simple to clean and a good form of energy conservation. Defrosting food, once a problem for every homemaker has now been made easy through the use of the microwave. It is now possible to take precooked food from your freezer, defrost and re-heat it in minutes. What a time saver!

There are many models of microwaves on the market to choose from, each with different features. After choosing the one that best suits your needs, read your instruction manual as to its proper care and use.

Utensils Recommended for Microwave Use

Most PYREX® and CORNING WARE® products
Glass
Plastic marked or labelled dishwasher safe
MICRO MAC® developed specifically for use in the microwave
Straw and Wicker — only for a few seconds for heating buns, bread or rolls
Metal utensils CANNOT be used. Metal reflects the microwaves and can cause arcing as well as slowing down of the cooking process.
Wood — microwaving may cause drying or cracking of steak boards or other wooden serving containers.

The recipes in this book have been tried and tested and adapted for cooking in the microwave, some of them old favorites cooked conventionally. Once you have learned the principles of microwave cooking and tried some of these recipes, you may wish to convert some of your own. Microwave cooking generally takes one quarter of the time of conventional cooking. When you see how simple it is, you won't want to cook any other way.

To my family, George, Kim, Jackie and Holly for all the help and encouragement they have given me.
Also, to the many students who suggested I compile these recipes and hints into a cookbook.

Ruby Schile Juss

Food pictured on front cover in a clockwise direction

Cornish Hens with Honey Marmalade Glaze page 97.
Bacon Wrapped Bread Sticks page 15.
Marinated Cauliflower page 13.
Cream Cheese Stuffed Mushroom Caps page 19.
French Beans with Bacon and Almonds page 40.

French Onion Soup page 26.

Flaming Cherries Jubilee page 121.

CONTENTS

Appetizers

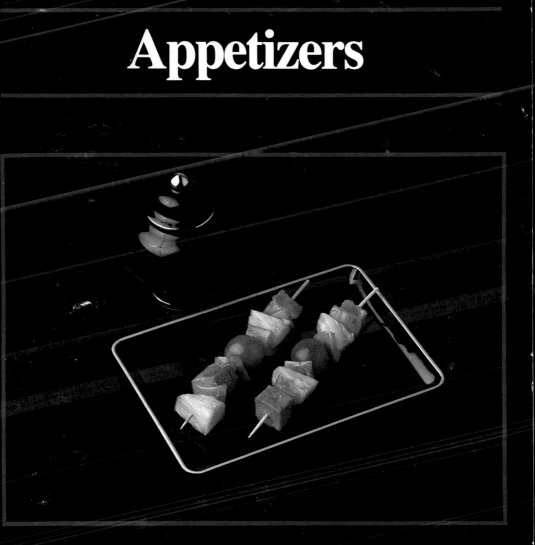

variety of appetizers can be prepared well in advance of serving. Pre-frozen ones are easily heated in the microwave and served piping hot to guests. A colorful selection can be cooked in the same serving container with decorative plastic or wooden picks to handle meats, vegetables and different types of kabobs.

Sweet and Sour Ham Kabobs page 20.

▤Italian Pizza On Melba Rounds

30	30	melba toast rounds
170mL	6	oz can tomato paste
		salami slices or pepperoni sausage, sliced thinly.
175 mL	¾	cup shredded mozzarella cheese
5 mL	1	teaspoon Italian seasoning spice

1. Spread tomato paste on each melba round.
2. Top each round with 1 slice of salami or pepperoni and ½-1 teaspoon (2-5 mL) shredded cheese. Sprinkle with Italian seasoning.
3. In a round microwave dish, place 10-12 crackers and microwave 30-60 seconds on *high*.
4. Don't cover crackers.
5. Serves 6-8.

Refreshen Snacks — Potato chips, pretzels, nuts and bolts, crackers and popcorn can be refreshened by microwaving for 30 seconds on *high* in a microproof container.

≡Cheese and Bacon Cracker Puffs

250 g	8	oz package softened cream cheese
1	1	egg yolk
5 mL	1	teaspoon dry minced onion
5 mL	1	teaspoon baking powder
35 mL	2½	Tablespoons cooked bacon pieces, crumbled. (see recipe below)
		Melba toast rounds or snack crackers

1. Combine cream cheese, egg yolk and dry minced onion in a large mixing bowl. Mix well.
2. Add baking powder and bacon crumbles. Mix well again.
3. Top each cracker with 1 teaspoon (5 mL) of cheese mixture.
4. Microwave 10-12 crackers, uncovered, 1-1½ minutes on *medium*. Serve hot.

Bacon Crumbles

Place 4 bacon slices on a paper lined plate, cover with paper towel, microwave 3 minutes on *high*. Let stand 3 minutes to crisp, then crumble the bacon.

Paper Towels and Napkins — Use only white as the dye from colored ones may go into the food. Recycled paper may ignite if used.

Sweet and Sour Cheese Dip

4	4	slices bacon
250 g	8	oz package cream cheese, softened
50 mL	¼	cup sweet and sour salad dressing, or Russian dressing
30 mL	2	Tablespoons milk

1. Microwave bacon 3 minutes on *high*.
2. Cool and crumble bacon into a bowl.
3. Combine cheese and salad dressing, in a medium size bowl. Beat until smooth.
4. Fold in bacon and chill for 2-4 hours.
5. Serve with crackers or crisp vegetables.

Marinated Cauliflower

1	1	small head cauliflower
250 mL	1	cup Italian or French dressing
dash		dash Tabasco sauce

1. Wash cauliflower and pat dry. Separate flowerettes into bite size pieces.
2. Combine dressing of your choice with Tabasco sauce.
3. Microwave dressing for 2-4 minutes on *high*. Pour hot dressing on cauliflower.
4. Refrigerate cauliflower and dressing overnight to allow flavor to penetrate.
5. Drain; serve with toothpicks.

▤Crumbed Cauliflower Pickups

1	1	small head cauliflower
125 mL	½	cup butter or margarine
125 mL	½	cup cornflake crumbs
50 mL	¼	cup Parmesan cheese
5 mL	1	teaspoon tarragon or parsley leaves
5 mL	1	teaspoon oregano spice
5 mL	1	teaspoon paprika
dash		dash of pepper

1. Wash cauliflower and pat dry. Separate flowerettes into bite size pieces.
2. Microwave butter in a small bowl for 1-1½ minutes or until melted.
3. Combine cornflake crumbs, cheese and spices in a plastic bag. Shake well.
4. Dip cauliflower pieces in butter and shake in crumb mixture to coat evenly.
5. Arrange flowerettes in a round 9″ (23 cm) microproof pie plate. Sprinkle with paprika, cover with paper towel and microwave 4-5 minutes on *high*.

Marinated Weiners

6	6	weiners, cut into 1″ pieces
125 mL	½	cup apricot jam
15 mL	1	Tablespoon prepared mustard

1. Mix together apricot jam and mustard.
2. Microwave mixture 2-3 minutes on high, stirring once.
3. Pour mixture over weiners, and let marinate 2-4 hours.
4. Place weiners in a round 9″ (23 cm) paper towel lined microproof pie plate.
5. Cover with paper towel and microwave 3-4 minutes on *high*.

Bacon Wrapped Bread Sticks

6	6	strips bacon
12	12	thin long dry bread sticks (any flavor)
50 mL	¼	cup soy sauce for flavor

1. Cut bacon in half lengthwise with scissors or a sharp knife.
2. Wrap one bacon slice in a spiral manner around a bread stick; looks like a candy cane, or barbers pole.
3. Brush with soy sauce for flavor and color.
4. Microwave on *high* 3-4 minutes on a paper towel lined microproof plate. Cover with a paper towel to absorb bacon grease.

≣ Crab Dip (Hot or Cold)

250 mL	8	oz package cream cheese
75 mL	⅓	cup mayonnaise
5 mL	1	teaspoon horseradish
20 mL	1½	Tablespoons minced onion or dried onions
15 mL	1	Tablespoon chopped dry parsley flakes
1 mL	¼	teaspoon seasoned salt
		sprinkle of garlic powder
170 g	6	oz can of crab meat

1. To soften cream cheese, microwave 20 seconds on *medium* heat in small microproof bowl.
2. Mix the cream cheese, add mayonnaise, horseradish, onion, seasoned salt, garlic powder and parsley flakes.
3. Rinse crab meat in cold water, drain. Stir into cream cheese mixture.
4. To heat; place ingredients in a microproof bowl, microwave 1-1½ minutes on *medium high* uncovered. Stir and microwave 1 minute longer.
5. Serve on crackers as this mixture is thick, or use as dip for vegetables.

 Popcorn — Pop popcorn only in a recommended microwave popcorn popper. DO NOT use brown paper bags or casserole dishes. Paper will ignite from the hot kernels and the oil in a casserole dish will become so hot that the kernels will burn.

≡Marinated Mushrooms

568 mL	2-4	(10 oz) cans whole mushrooms
125 mL	½	cup white sugar
125 mL	½	cup white vinegar
125 mL	½	cup vegetable oil
2 mL	½	teaspoon dry mustard
5 mL	1	teaspoon salt
2 mL	½	teaspoon pepper

1. Drain mushrooms
2. Combine sugar, vinegar, oil, mustard, salt and pepper in a 4 cup (1L) pyrex measuring pitcher.
3. Microwave ingredients for 2 minutes on *high*. Stir to dissolve sugar, and microwave 1-2 minutes to boil dressing mixture.
4. Pour hot mixture over mushrooms, cover and refrigerate for 4 hours or overnight.
5. Drain dressing and serve marinated mushrooms with tooth picks.

≡Basic Stuffed Mushroom Caps

24	24	medium mushrooms
4	4	slices chopped bacon
50 mL	¼	cup chopped onion or dried onion
250 mL	1	cup bread crumbs
50 mL	¼	cup dry parmesan cheese
1 mL	¼	teaspoon pepper
2 mL	½	teaspoon parsley flakes
30 mL	2	Tablespoons milk (optional)

1. Wash mushrooms, remove stems and pat dry.
2. Chop stems finely.
3. In a 4 cup (1 L) measuring pitcher combine stems, bacon and onion. Microwave 3-4 minutes on *high*, stirring at 2 minutes.
4. Mix bread crumbs, cheese, parsley flakes and pepper into the bacon mixture. Mix until bread crumbs are moist and stick together. Add milk if too dry.
5. Stuff mushroom caps and arrange in a microproof circular baking dish, lined with paper towel. Cover with paper towel and microwave 3-4 minutes on *high*.
6. Standing time: 2 minutes.

Cream Cheese Stuffed Mushrooms Caps

24	24	medium sized mushrooms
30 mL	2	Tablespoons butter or margarine
50 mL	¼	cup chopped onion or dry onion
125 g	4	oz package cream cheese
60 mL	4	Tablespoons fine bread crumbs
50 mL	¼	cup milk (optional)
15 mL	1	Tablespoon parsley

1. Wash mushrooms and remove stems. Pat dry.
2. Chop stems finely.
3. In a 4 cup (1L) measuring pitcher, combine butter, onion and stems. Microwave for 3-4 minutes on *high*, stirring once.
4. Stir in cheese and crumbs. Mix well until crumbs are moist. Add milk if too dry.
5. Spoon filling into each cap and arrange caps in a circle on a paper towel lined round 9" (23 cm) microproof pie plate. Sprinkle parsley flakes on the caps. Cover with paper towel.
6. Microwave 3-4 minutes on *high*.

 Softening Cream Cheese — Unwrap cream cheese and place in a microproof bowl, and microwave for 30 seconds to 1 minute on *medium*, uncovered.

≡Sweet and Sour Ham Kabobs

2	2	large green peppers, cut in chunks
454 g	1	pound ham cubes (breakfast canned or regular cooked ham)
397 g	1	can unsweetened pineapple chunks
125 mL	½	cup oriental plum sauce or sweet and sour sauce
15 mL	1	Tablespoon soy sauce, light or dark

1. Microwave green pepper chunks 2-3 minutes, to remove some of the crispness.
2. Alternate ham cubes, green pepper and pineapple chunks on skewers. Use small thin bamboo skewers, or use a thicker toothpick.
3. Mix together plum or sweet and sour sauce, and soy sauce. Brush on the kabobs.
4. Cover and microwave 4-5 minutes on *high* on a paper towel lined round microproof pie plate, 9″ (23cm).
5. Standing time 2 minutes.

 Bacon Bits — Place 2-3 slices of bacon on 2 layers of paper towel and microwave 2-3 minutes on *high*. Let stand 3 minutes to crisp, then crumble the bacon. Use to garnish your favorite recipes.

≡ Bacon Wrapped Water Chestnuts

6	6	slices of bacon, cut in half
227 g	8	oz can whole oriental water chestnuts
50 mL	¼	cup dark soy sauce
2 mL	½	teaspoon ginger powder
2 mL	½	teaspoon garlic powder

1. Microwave bacon slices for 3 minutes on *high*, on paper towelling, to remove extra fat.
2. Wrap a half slice of bacon around each water chestnut. Secure bacon with a tooth pick.
3. Marinate bacon-wrapped water chestnuts in soy sauce, garlic powder and ginger powder for 2-4 hours.
4. Arrange bacon-wrapped water chestnuts on a paper towel lined, round 9″ (23cm) microproof pie plate. Cover with paper towel.
5. Microwave 3 minutes on *high*.
6. Standing time 2 minutes.

Extra Bacon Wrap Suggestions

1. Pineapple chunks.
2. Green or black olives.
3. Canned whole mushrooms.
4. Chicken livers, cut into 1″ pieces.
5. Cooked shrimp.
5. Green peppers.
7. Brussel sprouts, cut in half.

▦Cranberry Sipper

1364 mL	48	oz can cranberry juice
125 mL	½	cup sugar
125 mL	½	cup red cinnamon candies or ¼ teaspoon (1 mL) cinnamon
500 mL	2	cups pineapple or orange juice
187 mL	¾	cup water
		orange slices, if desired
250 mL	1	cup red wine (optional)

1. In a microwave simmer pot, combine cranberry juice, candies or cinnamon, pineapple or orange juice, and water.
2. Cover and microwave on *high* for 5 minutes; stir to dissolve candies.
3. *Simmer* ingredients another 5-8 minutes. Stir, add red wine.
4. Serve with an orange slice.
5. Serves 6.

 Softening Dried Fruits — Add ¼ cup (50 mL) of water to fruit in a microproof casserole dish. Cover and microwave 2-3 minutes on *medium*.

Mulled Tomato Juice

1364 mL	48	oz can tomato juice
10 mL	2	teaspoons Worcestershire sauce
1 mL	¼	teaspoon salt
1 mL	¼	teaspoon celery salt
0.5 mL	⅛	teaspoon oregano leaves
3	3	drops tabasco sauce

1. Mix all ingredients in a simmer pot, microwave uncovered for 6-8 minutes on *high*.
2. Serve in cups. Garnish with celery sticks or green onions.
3. It can be served hot, or cold.
4. Serves 6.

Mulled Apple Cider

1364 mL	48	oz can apple cider or juice
50 mL	¼	cup brown sugar
4	4	broken up cinnamon sticks
6	6	whole cloves
1	1	orange, sliced
½	½	lemon, sliced
250 mL	1	cup white wine (optional)

1. In a microwave simmer pot, combine cider, brown sugar, cinnamon and cloves.
2. Cover and microwave on *high* for 10 minutes. Add white wine; stir.
3. Strain and serve hot.
4. Garnish with oranges or lemon slices.
5. Serves 6.

≡Mulled Apricot Nectar

1364 mL	48	oz can apricot nectar
250 mL	1	cup orange juice
4	4	broken up cinnamon sticks
1 mL	¼	teaspoon allspice
6	6	whole cloves
250 mL	1	cup rum (optional)
1	1	lemon, sliced (optional)

1. In a microwave simmer pot, combine apricot nectar, orange juice, cinnamon sticks, allspice, cloves.
2. Cover and microwave on *high* for 10 minutes. Add rum, stir.
3. Strain and serve with a lemon slice.
4. Serves 6.

Blanching Nuts — To blanch nuts with skins on (i.e. almonds or hazelnuts), cover with hot tap water. Cover and microwave 1 minute on high. Rinse with cold water. Peel skins.

▤Quick Tomato Consommé Soup

750 mL	3	cups tomato juice
284 mL	10	oz can beef consommé
15 mL	1	Tablespoon butter or margarine
1 mL	¼	teaspoon salt
1 mL	¼	teaspoon sugar
1 mL	¼	teaspoon pepper
1 mL	¼	teaspoon basil
10 mL	2	teaspoons lemon juice

1. Combine tomato juice, beef consommé, butter or margarine, lemon juice and seasonings into a microproof simmer pot.
2. Cover and microwave 10 minutes on *high*.
3. Serve as pre-dinner appetizer.
4. Makes 5-6 servings.

 Plastic Wrap — Vent plastic wrap by fan-folding a corner or by poking a few holes on top of wrapped cooking dish.

≡French Onion Soup

2	2	large onions, cut into strips
30 mL	2	Tablespoons butter or margarine
568 mL	2-	10 oz cans of beef broth, or consommé
568 mL	2-	10 oz cans of hot water
5 mL	1	teaspoon Worcestershire sauce
2 mL	½	teaspoon salt
1 mL	¼	teaspoon pepper
		toasted croutons
		grated Parmesan or mozzarella cheese

1. Combine onions and butter or margarine in a microproof simmer pot. Cover and microwave 5 minutes on *high*.
2. Add beef broth, water, Worcestershire sauce, salt and pepper. Cover and microwave 10-12 minutes on *high*.
3. Ladle soup into onion soup bowls. Sprinkle with croutons and cheese. Microwave each soup bowl 30 seconds until cheese melts.
4. Makes 5-6 servings.

 Croutons or Bread Crumbs — Cube bread to make 2 cups (500 mL) and place in a microproof shallow dish. Microwave 3-4 minutes on *high*.

Vegetables and Eggs

Vegetables cooked in a microwave are crisp, colorful, and retain their fresh taste. Vitamins and minerals are retained, due to the speed in cooking and minimum amount of water used.

Salt is used during standing time or if there is enough water used. Stir salt granules until they are dissolved.

Stir vegetables half way through cooking to eliminate overcooking the vegetables on the outer side of the dish.

Vegetables that are of the starch family or root vegetables require more water to cook after January, if they have been stored since fall.

Do not wrap whole potatoes in foil after they have been microwaved. This makes the potatoes too soggy. Wrap them in a dish towel or paper towel to absorb moisture.

Arrange flower-type vegetables by placing thick stalks to the outside of a microproof dish and flowerettes to the center.

When cooking potatoes or yams, pierce the skins as they may burst in the oven.

Cut vegetables such as carrots to uniform size, as they will cook more evenly. Large sizes may be undercooked and smaller ones over-cooked.

E ggs are a good source of protein and can be eaten during any meal of the day as a meat substitute.

The membranes on the egg yolk and white have to be pierced to eliminate bursting during cooking.

Seasoned Vegetable Platter page 37.
Poached Eggs Benedict page 44 with Hollandaise Sauce page 107.

E ggs are a good source of protein and can be eaten during any meal of the day as a meat substitute.

The membranes on the egg yolk and white have to be pierced to eliminate bursting during cooking.

Vegetables that are of the starch family or root vegetables require more water to cook after January, if they have been stored since fall.

Do not wrap whole potatoes in foil after they have been microwaved. This makes the potatoes too soggy. Wrap them in a dish towel or paper towel to absorb moisture.

Arrange flower-type vegetables by placing thick stalks to the outside of a microproof dish and flowerettes to the center.

When cooking potatoes or yams, pierce the skins as they may burst in the oven.

Cut vegetables such as carrots to uniform size, as they will cook more evenly. Large sizes may be undercooked and smaller ones over-cooked.

Seasoned Vegetable Platter page 37.
Poached Eggs Benedict page 44 with Hollandaise Sauce page 107.

Vegetables and Eggs

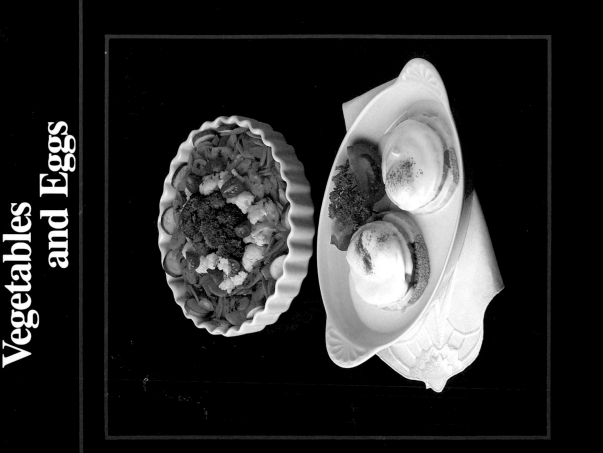

Vegetables cooked in a microwave are crisp, colorful, and retain their fresh taste. Vitamins and minerals are retained, due to the speed in cooking and minimum amount of water used.

Salt is used during standing time or if there is enough water used. Stir salt granules until they are dissolved.

Stir vegetables half way through cooking to eliminate overcooking the vegetables on the outer side of the dish.

≡Microwave Fried Potatoes

30 mL	2	Tablespoons cooking oil
4-6	4-6	medium potatoes peeled and sliced
1	1	medium sliced onion
1 mL	¼	teaspoon dill
1 mL	¼	teaspoon pepper
1 mL	¼	teaspoon paprika
2 mL	½	teaspoon salt

1. Preheat browning pan with 2 Tablespoons (30 mL) oil for 4 minutes on *high*.
2. Place potatoes, onion, dill and pepper in hot browning pan.
3. Cover and microwave 10 minutes on *high*. Stir well.
4. Cover and microwave 8-10 minutes on *high*, stir, then sprinkle with salt and paprika.
5. Standing time 5 minutes.
6. Serves 4-5.

≡Lemon Ginger Carrots

6	6	carrots sliced diagonally
50 mL	¼	cup water
63 mL	4	Tablespoons butter or margarine
15 mL	1	Tablespoon brown sugar or honey
15 mL	1	Tablespoon lemon juice
2 mL	½	teaspoon ginger powder
1 mL	¼	teaspoon salt
1 mL	¼	teaspoon pepper

1. In a 1 quart (1L) microproof casserole dish, microwave carrots and water for 10 minutes on *high*, stirring at 5 minutes.
2. In a 2 cup (500 mL) measuring pitcher, mix butter and margarine, brown sugar, lemon juice and seasonings and microwave 2 minutes on *high*.
3. Pour sauce over drained carrots, then microwave 2 minutes on *high*.
4. Standing time 4 minutes.
5. Serves 4-5.

Scalloped Potatoes

4	4	medium potatoes, sliced thinly
125 mL	½	cup chopped onion
375 mL	1½	cups milk or half and half cream
30 mL	2	Tablespoons flour, if using milk
2 mL	½	teaspoon salt
1 mL	¼	teaspoon pepper
30 mL	2	Tablespoons butter or margarine
30 mL	2	Tablespoons shredded Cheddar cheese (optional)
		Sprinkle of paprika or parsley flakes

1. Alternate sliced potatoes and onions in a 2 quart (2L) microproof casserole dish.
2. Mix milk, flour, salt and pepper into a 4 cup (1L) measuring pitcher. Microwave 2 minutes on *high*, stirring well. Microwave 1 minute on *high* until hot.
3. Dot potatoes with butter and pour milk mixture over potatoes.
4. Cover and slightly vent to prevent over-boiling of milk. Microwave 10 minutes on *high* and stir. Partly cover and microwave 10 minutes on *high*.
5. Sprinkle with cheese, paprika or parsley flakes.
6. Standing time 5 minutes.
7. Serves 4-5.

Harvard Beets

4	4	medium beets, washed and topped
250 mL	1	cup hot water

1. Place whole beets in a 2 quart (2L) microproof casserole dish.
2. Cover and microwave 10-12 minutes on *high* or until fork-tender.
3. Place cooked beets in cold water. Peel, slice or cube.

Sauce

15-30 mL	1-2	Tablespoons cornstarch or tapioca starch
15 mL	1	Tablespoon sugar
2 mL	½	teaspoon salt
1 mL	¼	teaspoon pepper
50 mL	¼	cup vinegar
166 mL	⅔	cup water

1. Combine cornstarch or tapioca starch, sugar, salt, pepper, vinegar and water in a 2 cup (500 mL) measuring pitcher. Mix well.
2. Microwave 4 minutes on *high*, stirring at 2 minutes. Cook until thickened.
3. Place sliced beets in a 2 quart (2L) microproof casserole dish and pour sauce over beets
4. Cover and microwave 3-4 minutes on *high*.
5. Standing time 2 minutes.
6. Serves 4-5.

▤Quick Corn Casserole

30 mL	2	Tablespoons butter or margarine
1	1	egg
125 mL	½	cup soda cracker crumbs
398 mL	14	oz can cream style corn
15 mL	1	Tablespoon dry onion
1 mL	¼	teaspoon salt
1 mL	¼	teaspoon pepper

1. In a 1 quart (1L) microproof casserole dish, microwave butter or margarine for 30 seconds on *high*.
2. Add egg, cracker crumbs, corn, onion, salt and pepper. Blend evenly.
3. Cover and microwave 4-6 minutes on *high*, stirring at 4 minutes.
4. Standing time 5 minutes.
5. Serves 4.

▤Broccoli Italienne

1 kg	2	pounds fresh broccoli or 2-10 oz packages frozen broccoli spears
50 mL	¼	cup water
125 mL	½	cup mayonnaise
30 mL	¼	cup shredded sharp Cheddar cheese
15-30 mL	1-2	Tablespoons milk
2 mL	½	teaspoon salt
2 mL	½	teaspoon oregano

1. Place broccoli in a 2 quart (2L) microproof casserole dish. Add ¼ cup (50 mL) water if fresh broccoli is used. No water is necessary if broccoli is frozen. Cover and microwave 10 minutes on *high*.
2. Mix mayonnaise, cheese, milk, salt and oregano in a 2 cup (500 mL) measuring pitcher. Microwave 1 minute on *medium*, stir, and microwave on *medium* until cheese is melted.
3. Drizzle over broccoli.
4. Serves 4-5.

▤Stuffed Tomatoes

8	8	ripe tomatoes
4	4	slices bacon, chopped
50 mL	¼	cup chopped onion
50 mL,	¼	cup chopped celery
30 mL	2	Tablespoons melted butter or margarine
250 mL	1	cup bread crumbs
15 mL	1	Tablespoon warm water
1 mL	¼	teaspoon parsley flakes
1 mL	¼	teaspoon garlic powder
1 mL	¼	teaspoon salt
1 mL	¼	teaspoon pepper

1. Remove stem ends of tomatoes and scoop out part of centre pulp and seeds. Place tomatoes in a round 9" (23 cm) microproof baking dish.
2. In a 4 cup (1L) measuring pitcher, microwave bacon, onion, celery and butter or margarine, for 5-6 minutes on *high*.
3. Stir in bread crumbs, water and seasonings.
4. Spoon stuffing into tomatoes. Cover and microwave 3-4 minutes on *high* or until tomatoes are heated.
5. Serves 8.

 Oil and Fat — Microwave cooking steam cooks; therefore low-calorie foods may be cooked without fats or oils.

≡Stuffed Zucchini

4	4	zucchini, cut in half lengthwise
30 mL	2	Tablespoons melted butter or margarine
4	4	slices chopped bacon
50 mL	¼	cup chopped onion
50 mL	¼	cup chopped celery
125 mL	½	cup chopped mushrooms
1	1	small chopped tomato
250 mL	1	cup bread crumbs
15 mL	1	Tablespoon warm water
1 mL	¼	teaspoon salt
1 mL	¼	teaspoon pepper
1 mL	¼	teaspoon paprika
50 mL	¼	cup shredded Cheddar cheese

1. Scoop pulp out of the zucchini and chop coarsely. Combine butter or margarine, bacon, onion, celery, mushrooms and tomatoes in a microproof 2 quart (2L) casserole dish. Cover and microwave 5-6 minutes on *high*, stirring once. Drain if necessary.
2. Stir in bread crumbs, water and seasonings into ingredients.
3. Spoon filling into each zucchini and place in microproof 9″ x 9″ (2.5L) baking dish. Cover with plastic wrap, vent and microwave 5-7 minutes on *high*.
4. Sprinkle Cheddar cheese on zucchini. Uncover and microwave 2-3 minutes on *high* or until cheese melts.
5. Standing time 2-4 minutes.
6. Serves 8.

≡Stuffed Green Peppers

4-5	4-5	green peppers, cored and seeded
454 g	1	pound ground beef
125 mL	½	cup chopped onions
50 mL	¼	cup chopped celery
250 mL	1	cup rice, precooked (or minute rice)
1 mL	¼	teaspoon garlic powder
2 mL	½	teaspoon salt
1 mL	¼	teaspoon pepper
568 mL	2-	10 oz cans tomato soup

1. Cut peppers in half lengthwise. Place peppers in an 8" x 8" (2L) microproof baking dish.
2. Crumble hamburger in a 2 quart (2L) casserole dish. Add onions and celery. Cover and microwave 3-4 minutes on *high*. Stir at 2 minutes.
3. Drain fat. Add remaining ingredients to hamburger with ½ can (142 mL) tomato soup. Mix together well.
4. Fill peppers with stuffing mixture. Add remaining tomato soup on top of stuffed peppers. Add enough soup to cover peppers. Cover dish with plastic wrap.
5. Cover and microwave 10-12 minutes on *high* or until peppers are tender crisp.
6. Standing time 5 minutes.
7. Serves 4-5.

Vegetables for Stew — Pre-cook your vegetables in the microwave when preparing a stew. Cover the vegetables and cook 5 minutes on high.

▤Basic Cabbage Rolls with Dill

Core whole cabbage and microwave in a 4 quart (4L) casserole dish with boiling water for 3-5 minutes on *high*, until leaves separate. The leaves stay nice and green.

Filling

454 g	1	pound ground hamburger
50 mL	¼	cup onion
250 mL	1	cup cooked rice
1 mL	¼	teaspoon dill
15 mL	1	teaspoon salt
1 mL	¼	teaspoon pepper
284 mL	1-	10 oz can tomato soup or sauce
398 mL	1-	14 oz can stewed tomatoes
15 mL	1	Tablespoon brown sugar, optional

1. In a 4 quart (4L) casserole dish, crumble ground beef and add onions cover and microwave 3-4 minutes on *high* till pinkness of meat is gone.
2. Drain fat. Add rice, dill, salt, pepper and ½ can (142 mL) tomato soup, into cooked hamburger.
3. Place beef-rice filling into cabbage leaf, roll up, folding edges in. Arrange cabbage rolls in a 9″ x 9″ (2.5L) baking dish.
4. Mix remaining tomato soup with stewed tomatoes, add brown sugar and pour over cabbage rolls.
5. Cover with wax paper. Microwave 10 minutes on *high*. Turn cabbage rolls over. Cover and microwave another 10 minutes on *high*.
6. Standing time 5-6 minutes.
7. Serves 5-6.

≡Seasoned Vegetable Platter

500 mL	2	cups thinly sliced carrots
500 mL	2	cups broccoli flowerettes
500 mL	2	cups cauliflowerettes
1	1	zucchini, thinly sliced
50 mL	¼	cup hot water
1	1	tomato cut into wedges

1. Arrange vegetables in a round 9″ (23 cm) microproof baking dish, beginning with carrots to outside of dish, broccoli and cauliflower, facing towards centre of dish, with zucchini in centre of dish.
2. Sprinkle tray with water. Cover with plastic wrap. Vent and microwave 10 minutes on *high*.
3. Arrange tomato wedges over vegetables. Cover and microwave 2 minutes on *high*.
4. During standing time of 4 minutes, prepare sauce.

Sauce

30 mL	2	Tablespoons butter or margarine
15 mL	1	Tablespoon lemon juice
1 mL	¼	teaspoon salt
1 mL	¼	teaspoon pepper
1 mL	¼	teaspoon parsley flakes
15 mL	1	Tablespoon parmesan cheese

1. Melt butter or margarine in a 2 cup (500 mL) measuring pitcher. Add lemon juice, salt, pepper and parsley flakes. Stir well.
2. Drain vegetables, sprinkle with Parmesan cheese then drizzle with melted butter and seasoning mixture.
3. Serves 6-8.

≡Zucchini Tomato Cheese Casserole

750 mL	3	cups sliced zucchini
250 mL	1	cup sliced onion
15 mL	1	Tablespoon butter or margarine
1 mL	¼	teaspoon oregano
1 mL	¼	teaspoon marjoram
1 mL	¼	teaspoon garlic powder
1 mL	¼	teaspoon salt
1 mL	¼	teaspoon pepper
1	1	sliced tomato
30 mL	2	Tablespoon Parmesan cheese

1. Combine zucchini, onion and butter or margarine, in a 2 quart (2L) microproof casserole dish. Sprinkle oregano, marjoram, garlic powder, salt and pepper.
2. Cover and microwave 5-6 minutes on *high*.
3. Stir and place tomato slices on top of zucchini. Sprinkle with Parmesan cheese.
4. Cover and microwave 4 minutes on *high*.
5. Standing time 2-4 minutes.
6. Serves 4-5.

 Canned Vegetables — Drain the liquid and save it for soups or gravies. Vegetables heated without liquid heat faster in the microwave.

≡ Creamed Onions

4	4	large onions cut in quarters
30 mL	¼	cup water
1 mL	¼	teaspoon salt

1. Place quartered onions into a 2 quart (2L) microproof casserole dish.
2. Add water, cover and microwave 5 minutes on *high*.
3. Stir onions, cover and microwave 5 minutes on *high*. Add salt during standing time.

Basic White Sauce

30 mL	2	Tablespoons butter or margarine
30 mL	2	Tablespoons flour
2 mL	½	teaspoon salt
1 mL	¼	teaspoon white pepper
250 mL	1	cup milk

1. Melt butter in a 2 cup (500 mL) measuring pitcher for 30 seconds on *medium high*.
2. Stir flour, salt and pepper into the liquid margarine or butter.
3. Gradually add milk, stirring until smooth.
4. Cook uncovered 3-4 minutes on *medium high*, until sauce is thickened. Stir sauce at least twice.
5. Pour over onions, stir well.
6. Serves 4-6.

≡French Beans with Bacon and Almonds

568 mL	2-	10 oz packages frozen french cut beans or
500-1000g	1-2	pounds fresh beans frenched
4	4	slices cooked and crumbled bacon
5 mL	1	teaspoon butter or margarine
2 mL	½	teaspoon salt
50 mL	¼	cup slivered almonds

1. Place frozen french beans into a 2 qt. (2L) microproof casserole dish with 2 Tablespoons (30 mL) of water; or when using fresh french beans use ½ cup (125 mL) of water.
2. Cover and microwave 6 minutes on *high*. Stir well, cover and microwave 6 minutes more on *high*. If beans feel tough, stir again, cover and microwave another 5 minutes on *high*.
3. Drain beans, add butter or margarine, salt, crumbled bacon and almonds. Cover and microwave 3 minutes on *high*. Standing time 2-4 minutes.
4. Serves 4-6.

Tip

Chopped onions can be added to bacon and almonds. Microwave for a total of 5 minutes instead of 3 minutes.

▤Quick Potato Salad

3-4	3-4	medium peeled potatoes
50 mL	¼	cup hot water
50 mL	3	Tablespoons chopped celery
50 mL	3	Tablespoons chopped green onion
2	2	hard boiled eggs chopped (cooked conventionally)
4	4	sliced radishes
250 mL	1	cup mayonnaise or salad dressing
2 mL	½	teaspoon salt
1 mL	¼	teaspoon pepper
1 mL	¼	teaspoon dry mustard

1. Cut peeled potatoes into one inch (2.2 cm) cubes. Place cubed potatoes into a 2 quart (2L) microwave proof casserole dish. Add hot water.
2. Cover and microwave 5 minutes on *high*. Stir. Cover and microwave another 5 minutes on *high*.
3. Drain and cool potatoes at least 30 minutes.
4. Place potatoes into a salad bowl, add celery, onions, eggs and radishes.
5. Mix mayonnaise or salad dressing, salt, pepper and dry mustard into a mixing bowl. Mix well. Spoon mayonnaise mixture over vegetables tossing to coat.
6. Serves 4-6.

Frozen Vegetables — Frozen vegetables can be microwaved in plastic pouches or boil-in-bags. Make a slit in the plastic to let steam escape during cooking. Use rubber bands, string or plastic bread fasteners, instead of twist ties to secure bags during cooking. Twist ties do cause sparking and arcing.

▤Microwave Rice

500 mL	2	cups hot water.
2 mL	½	teaspoon salt
15 mL	1	Tablespoon butter or margarine or cooking oil
250 mL	1	cup raw rice

1. Mix hot water, salt, butter or margarine and rice into a microproof simmer pot. Stir well.
2. Cover and slightly vent lid. Microwave 5 minutes on *high*.
3. Stir rice, cover and microwave 5-6 minutes on *high*.
4. Standing time 5 minutes.

▤Popular Quiche Lorraine

Crust

500 mL	2	cups dry, fine bread crumbs
125 mL	½	cup melted butter or margarine
1 mL	¼	teaspoon pepper

1. Combine bread crumbs, melted butter or margarine and pepper. Mix and press into a 9″ (23 cm) microproof quiche dish or pie plate.
2. Microwave crust 2 minutes on *medium*.

Topping

6	6	strips cooked bacon, crumbled.
125 mL	½	cup grated Swiss or mozzarella cheese
3-4	3-4	chopped green onions
20 mL	1½	Tablespoons flour
1 mL	¼	teaspoon salt
1 mL	¼	teaspoon pepper
0.5 mL	⅛	teaspoon cayenne
1 mL	¼	teaspoon nutmeg
250 mL	1	cup whipping cream or half and half cream
250 mL	1	cup milk
4	4	eggs
		dash of paprika

1. Save 2 Tablespoons of each; bacon, cheese, and onion.
2. Sprinkle bacon, cheese and onion over bread crumb crust.
3. Combine flour, salt, pepper, cayenne and nutmeg into a 4 cup (1L) measuring pitcher. Gradually stir in cream and milk. Microwave 6-8 minutes on *medium*. Stirring every 2 minutes.
4. Beat eggs well and stir into hot liquid.
5. Microwave 2-4 minutes on *high*, stirring every minute until mixture thickens. Pour into crust, then top with remaining bacon, onion and cheese. Sprinkle on paprika.
6. Microwave 10-12 minutes on *medium* or until set.
7. Standing time 5 minutes.
8. Serves 4 6.

Variations

Instead of bacon use one of the following:

125 mL	½	cup shrimp
125 mL	½	cup crab
125 mL	½	cup ham
125 mL	½	cup chicken
125 mL	½	cup mushrooms
125 mL	½	cup onions

≡Poached Eggs Benedict

4	4	slices cooked ham
4	4	English muffins, split and toasted
4	4	eggs
3 mL	½	teaspoon vinegar
500 mL	2	cups water

1. Bring water and vinegar to a boil in a 1 quart (1L) microproof casserole dish. This will take 2-3 minutes on *high*.
2. Carefully crack each egg into the boiling water. Prick each egg yolk with a fork.
3. Cover with plastic wrap and microwave 2-3 minutes on *high*.
4. Standing time 2-3 minutes. If you prefer a firmer egg, let stand a little longer.
5. Place toasted muffin on plate, top with ham, poached egg and hollandaise sauce. See page 107.
6. Serves 4.

 Softening Butter — Soften ¼ pound (250 g) of butter or margarine in a microproof dish. Microwave for 30 seconds on *defrost*.

Meat

The following recipes have been very successfully done in the microwave. If you do not have a browning pan, meats with sauces do not have to be prebrowned. Meats that are cooked longer than 10-12 minutes will start to brown on their own. Glazes, bacon strips, browning agents, soup mixtures and melted butter or margarine with paprika added, enhance the browning of beef and pork roast.

Cooking Suggestions

Purchase meat in uniform shapes and sizes. Use foil, shiny side up, near the bone area or irregular shapes of the meat, during the first 15 minutes of cooking to eliminate overcooking of these areas. Elevate beef or pork roasts on a microproof meat rack or use an inverted saucer so that the meat is not sitting in its own fat and juices. Drain juices as they accumulate, and save for gravy. Turn meat over when microwaved half way through cooking time. This gives the meat even heating. Slower cooking tenderizes tougher cuts of meat. Cover with a tight lid and microwave on medium heat. Use meat marinade to tenderize beef and pork, but use salt during standing time only. If salt is sprinkled on meat during microwaving, the meat will become tough and dry.

To test meat for doneness, use a meat thermometer being sure the meat is outside of the microwave, as some meat thermometers are not microwave proof.

from the top in a counter-clockwise direction

Meat

The following recipes have been very successfully done in the microwave. If you do not have a browning pan, meats with sauces do not have to be prebrowned. Meats that are cooked longer than 10-12 minutes will start to brown on their own. Glazes, bacon strips, browning agents, soup mixtures and melted butter or margarine with paprika added, enhance the browning of beef and pork roast.

Cooking Suggestions

Purchase meat in uniform shapes and sizes. Use foil, shiny side up, near the bone area or irregular shapes of the meat, during the first 15 minutes of cooking to eliminate overcooking of these areas. Elevate beef or pork roasts on a microproof meat rack or use an inverted saucer so that the meat is not sitting in its own fat and juices. Drain juices as they accumulate, and save for gravy. Turn meat over when microwaved half way through cooking time. This gives the meat even heating. Slower cooking tenderizes tougher cuts of meat. Cover with a tight lid and microwave on medium heat. Use meat marinade to tenderize beef and pork, but use salt during standing time only. If salt is sprinkled on meat during microwaving, the meat will become tough and dry.

To test meat for doneness, use a meat thermometer being sure the meat is outside of the microwave, as some meat thermometers are not microwave proof.

46

≣Spicy Italian Pork Chops

30 mL	2	Tablespoons Cooking Oil
5-6	5-6	loin pork chops
1 mL	¼	teaspoon garlic powder
284 mL	10	oz can tomato soup or tomato sauce
50 mL	¼	cup water
1 mL	¼	teaspoon basil
0.5 mL	⅛	teaspoon pepper
		Pinch of thyme or oregano

1. Heat browning pan with 2 Tablespoons (30 mL) oil for 4 minutes on *high*.
2. Sprinkle pork shops with garlic powder, cover and microwave pork chops for 4 minutes on *high*
3. Mix tomato soup or sauce with water and add dry seasoning to mixture. Cover and microwave in a 2 quart (2L) casserole dish for 5 minutes on *medium high*. Stir sauce at 3 minutes.
4. Pour sauce over pork chops. Cover and microwave for 15 minutes on *medium*. Turn pork chops at 7 minutes and stir sauce.

Waxed Paper — Waxed paper may be used to cover different dishes, but the wax may melt to fatty meats if touching.

≡Veal and Pork Scallopini

4-5	4-5	pork chops or veal
1	1	beaten egg
500 mL	2	cups bread crumbs mixed with corn flake crumbs
2 mL	½	teaspoon salt
1 mL	¼	teaspoon pepper
1 mL	¼	teaspoon garlic powder
30 mL	2	Tablespoons cooking oil
30 mL	2	Tablespoons butter or margarine
30 mL	2	Tablespoons flour
125 mL	½	cup white wine
250 mL	1	cup vegetable stock or milk
250 mL	1	cup sliced fresh mushrooms or
284 mL	10	oz can sliced mushrooms

1. Dip chops or veal in beaten egg and coat with crumb mixture. Sprinkle seasonings on chops or veal.
2. Preheat browning pan with 2 Tablespoons (30 mL) oil for 4 minutes on *high*.
3. Place chops or veal into browning pan. Cover and microwave 10 minutes on *medium*.
4. Turn chops or veal over and microwave 5 minutes on *high*, uncovered.

Sauce

1. Melt butter or margarine in a 4 cup (1L) measuring pitcher. Mix flour into butter or margarine. Sir in wine and stock gradually.
2. Add mushrooms and microwave 4 minutes on *medium*, stirring at 2 minutes.
3. Pour sauce over veal or pork chops.
4. Standing time 2-4 minutes.

▤Pork Chop Suey

30 mL	2	Tablespoons cooking oil
454 g	1	pound pork, cut into strips
125 mL	½	cup sliced onion
125 mL	½	cup chopped celery
284 mL	10	oz can sliced mushrooms, drained
1	1	medium sliced green pepper
250 mL	1	cup fresh bean sprouts
227 mL	8	oz can sliced water chestnuts
2 mL	½	teaspoon salt
1 mL	¼	teaspoon pepper
1 mL	¼	teaspoon ginger
50 mL	¼	cup water
30 mL	2	Tablespoons cornstarch or tapioca starch
30-50 mL	2-3	Tablespoons soy sauce

1. Heat browning pan with 2 Tablespoons (30 mL) oil for 4 minutes on *high*.
2. Cover and microwave pork strips for 4 minutes on *high*. Stir at 2 minutes.
3. Add onion, celery, mushrooms, green pepper, bean sprouts and chestnuts. Sprinkle with salt, pepper and ginger. Cover and microwave 8-10 minutes on *high*.
4. Mix water, cornstarch or tapioca starch and soy sauce. Pour over meat and vegetables.
5. Cover and microwave 4 minutes on *high*, stirring once.
6. Standing time 2-5 minutes.
7. Serve with rice or Chinese noodles.

▤Pork and Pepper Supreme

30 mL	2	Tablespoons cooking oil
454 g	1	pound lean pork, cut into strips
1	1	medium pepper, seeded and cut in strips
284 mL	10	oz can sliced mushrooms
1	1	medium chopped onion
250 mL	1	cup tomato juice
5 mL	1	teaspoon Worcestershire sauce
2 mL	½	teaspoon horseradish
2 mL	½	teaspoon salt
1 mL	¼	teaspoon pepper
30 mL	2	Tablespoons cornstarch

1. Heat browning pan with 2 Tablespoons (30 mL) oil for 4 minutes on *high*.
2. Cover and microwave pork 4-5 minutes on *high*. Stir at 3 minutes.
3. Add green pepper, mushrooms and onion. Cover and microwave 5 minutes on *high*.
4. Mix tomato juice, Worcestershire sauce, horseradish, salt and pepper with cornstarch. Add to meat mixture, cover and microwave 8-10 minutes on *high*.
5. Standing time 5 minutes. Serve on rice.

▤Sweet and Sour Pork

30 mL	2	Tablespoons cooking oil
731 g	1½	pounds pork, sliced into strips
397 g	14	oz can pineapple chunks (save juice)
50 mL	¼	cup chopped onion
1	1	medium green pepper cut into chunks
50 mL	¼	cup brown sugar
50 mL	¼	cup white vinegar
50-65 mL	3-4	Tablespoons soy sauce
1 mL	¼	teaspoon salt
1 mL	¼	teaspoon ginger powder
30 mL	2	Tablespoons cornstarch or tapioca starch

1. Heat browning pan with 2 Tablespoons (30 mL) oil for 4 minutes on *high*.
2. Cover and microwave pork strips for 4 minutes on *high*. Stir and add pineapple chunks, onions and green pepper.
3. Combine brown sugar, vinegar, pineapple juice, soy sauce, salt, ginger powder and cornstarch. Mix well, and pour over meat.
4. Cover and microwave for 14 minutes on *medium high*. Stir at 7 minutes.
5. Standing time 5 minutes.
6. Serve on rice.

Foil — Use only a heavy duty foil. If foil is too light in weight, the stir fan may blow the foil against the microwave, causing arching or marring of the microwave.

≡Pork and Cabbage

681 g	1½	pounds pork, cut into strips
5 mL	1	teaspoon sugar
2 mL	½	teaspoon salt
15 mL	1	Tablespoon white cooking wine
50-60 mL	3-4	Tablespoons soy sauce
30 mL	2	Tablespoons cooking oil
1 mL	¼	teaspoon garlic powder
750 mL-1L	3-4	cups chopped cabbage
1 mL	¼	teaspoon pepper

1. Marinate pork with sugar, salt, wine and 2 Tablespoons soy sauce. Marinate ½-1 hour.
2. Heat browning pan with 2 Tablespoons (30 mL) oil for 4 minutes on *high*.
3. Cover and microwave pork strips sprinkled with garlic powder for 4 minutes on *high*.
4. Add cabbage, pepper and remaining soy sauce. Cover and microwave 10 minutes on *high*. Stir at 5 minutes.
5. Standing time 2-5 minutes.

Pork Chops with Mushroom Soup

30 mL	2	Tablespoons cooking oil
5-6	5-6	fast fry pork chops
284 mL	1-	10 oz can mushroom soup
284 mL	1	can sliced mushrooms
1 mL	¼	teaspoon pepper
1 mL	¼	teaspoon garlic powder
1 mL	¼	teaspoon sage powder
1 mL	¼	teaspoon salt
50 mL	¼	cup water

1. Heat browning pan with 2 Tablespoons (30 mL) oil for 4 minutes on *high*.
2. Cover and microwave pork chops 4 minutes on *high*. Turn pork chops over and drain fat.
3. Add mushroom soup, sliced mushrooms, seasoning and water.
4. Cover and microwave 10-12 minutes on *medium high*.
5. Stir soup and turn pork chops once during cooking.
6. Standing time 5 minutes.

Warming Left Overs — When warming a plate of left-overs, place dense or thick portions to outside edge of plate. Place delicate foods (mashed potatoes, vegetables) in center of plate. Cover with waxed paper or paper towel. Microwave 2-3 minutes on high.

▉Ham Broccoli Rolls in Mustard Sauce

6	6	thin slices of ham
6	6	large cooked broccoli spears
15 mL	1	Tablespoon butter or margarine
30 mL	2	Tablespoons flour
5 mL	1	teaspoon dry mustard
1 mL	¼	teaspoon salt
1 mL	¼	teaspoon pepper
250 mL	1	cup milk
1 mL	¼	teaspoon paprika

1. Put a broccoli spear into centre of each ham slice. Roll up tightly and arrange in a microproof 9" x 9" (2.5L) baking dish.
2. In a 4 cup (1L) measuring pitcher, melt butter and margarine for 30 seconds on *high*.
3. Blend in flour, mustard, salt and pepper. Slowly add milk, stirring until smooth. Microwave 2-4 minutes on *medium* until thickened.
4. Pour on ham rolls and sprinkle lightly with paprika. Cover with wax paper and microwave 6-8 minutes on *medium*.
5. Standing time 4 minutes.

☰Ground Ham and Noodle Casserole

284 mL	10	oz can of mushroom soup or celery soup
125 mL	½	cup milk
125 mL	½	cup sour cream
284 mL	10	oz can sliced mushrooms, drained
5 mL	1	teaspoon parsley flakes
500 mL	2	cups ground ham
1-1.25L	5-6	cups cooked noodles
175 mL	¾	cup cornflake crumbs
15 mL	1	Tablespoon melted butter or margarine
15 mL	1	Tablespoon grated cheddar cheese

1. In a large bowl stir together soup, milk, sour cream. Add mushroom slices, parsley flakes, ham and noodles.
2. Mix and place mixture into a 3 qt. (3L) casserole dish. Cover and microwave 10-12 minutes on *high*. Stir at 5-6 minutes.
3. Combine cornflake crumbs and melted butter or margarine. Sprinkle crumbs and cheese over casserole. Microwave 2 minutes on *high*.

☰Saturday Night For Beans

398 mL	14	oz can chunky pineapple, drained (reserve juice)
796 mL	28	oz can pork and beans
500 mL	2	cups chopped or sliced wieners, ham, spork or sausage
2 mL	½	teaspoon dry mustard
30 mL	2	Tablespoons molasses
15 ml.	1	Tablespoon brown sugar
30 mL	2	Tablespoons ketchup
		dash of pepper and salt

1. Combine pineapple, pork and beans, and your choice of meat, into a 4 quart (4L) casserole dish. Mix well.
2. Blend in a small bowl, pineapple juice, mustard, molasses, brown sugar and ketchup. Pour into beans and meat mixture.
3. Cover and microwave 10-12 minutes on *medium*. Stir at 6 minutes.
4. Salt and pepper to taste. Standing time 5 minutes.
5. Serve with salad and buns.

Chinese Style Liver and Peppers

30 mL	2	Tablespoons cooking oil
454 g	1	pound beef liver, cut into ½″ strips
2	2	green peppers, seeded and cut into strips
1	1	large onion, sliced thin
2 mL	½	teaspoon salt
1 mL	¼	teaspoon pepper
15-30 mL	1-2	Tablespoons cornstarch or tapioca starch
30 mL	2	Tablespoons soy sauce
250 mL	1	cup beef bouillon

1. Heat browning pan with 2 Tablespoons (30 mL) oil for 4 minutes on *high*.
2. Microwave liver 4-5 minutes on *high*. Stir at 3 minutes.
3. Add peppers, onion, salt and pepper.
4. Cover and microwave 5-6 minutes on *high*, stirring at 3 minutes.
5. Mix cornstarch, soy sauce and beef bouillon together. Pour into liver and stir. Cover and microwave 10 minutes on *high*, or until liver and vegetables are tender.
6. Standing time 5 minutes.
7. Serve on rice.

≡Oriental Beef and Broccoli

30 mL	2	Tablespoons cooking oil
731 g	1½	pounds round or sirloin steak, cut into strips
		Marinate steak 2-4 hours in:
25-50 mL	2-4	Tablespoons soy sauce
1 mL	¼	teaspoon ginger powder
1 mL	¼	teaspoon garlic powder
500-750 mL	2-3	cups broccoli flowerettes
125 mL	½	cup beef broth (1 bouillon cube dissolved in hot water)
15-30 mL	1-2	Tablespoons white cooking wine
30-50 mL	2-3	Tablespoons cornstarch or tapioca starch
30 mL	2	Tablespoons soy sauce
		Toasted sesame seeds

1. Preheat browning dish with 2 Tablespoons (30 mL) of oil, for 4 minutes on *high*.
2. Cover and microwave beef strips 5-7 minutes on *high*, stirring once at 3 minutes.
3. Add broccoli flowerettes. Cover and microwave 5-6 minutes on *high* until broccoli is tender. Stir once.
4. Blend together beef broth, cooking wine, cornstarch or tapioca starch and soy sauce. Pour onto steak and broccoli. Microwave 3-4 minutes on *high*, until sauce is thickened.
5. Sprinkle with sesame seeds.
6. Standing time 4-5 minutes.

≣Ginger Beef

30 mL	2	Tablespoons cooking oil
731 g	1½	pounds sirloin or round steak, cut into strips
1	1	medium green pepper cut into strips
1	1	medium onion, sliced
284 mL	10	oz can sliced mushrooms
1 mL	¼	teaspoon ginger
1 mL	¼	teaspoon garlic powder
1 mL	¼	teaspoon salt
125 mL	½	cup water
30 mL	2	Tablespoons soy sauce
30 mL	2	Tablespoons cornstarch or tapioca starch
1	1	tomato, cut in wedges

1. Heat browning pan with 2 Tablespoons (30 mL) oil for 4 minutes on *high*.
2. Cover and microwave steak strips 4 minutes on *high*. Stir.
3. Add green pepper, onion, sliced mushrooms, ginger, garlic powder and salt.
4. Cover and microwave 5-6 minutes on *high*. Stir once at 3 minutes.
5. Mix water, soy sauce, with cornstarch or tapioca starch. Pour into steak mixture. Microwave 4 minutes on *high*, until sauce thickens. Place tomato wedges on meat and microwave 2 minutes.
6. Standing time 5 minutes. Serve with rice.

▤Oriental Beef and Tomato

30 mL	2	Tablespoons cooking oil
454-908 g	1-2	pounds round or sirloin steak, cut into strips
		Marinate Steak 2-4 hours in:
30 mL	2	Tablespoons sugar
125 mL	½	cup soy sauce
1 mL	¼	teaspoon garlic powder
1 mL	¼	teaspoon ginger powder
2	2	medium green peppers, cut into strips
4	4	green onions, cut into 1 inch pieces
3	3	large tomatoes, cut into wedges
30-50 mL	2-3	Tablespoons cornstarch or tapioca starch
50 mL	¼	cup water

1. Preheat browning dish with 2 Tablespoons (30 mL) of oil, for 4 minutes on *high*.
2. Cover and microwave beef strips 5-7 minutes on *high*, stirring once at 3 minutes.
3. Drain cooking juices into marinade.
4. Stir green pepper and onion into meat, cover and microwave 5-6 minutes on *high*, stirring once at 3 minutes. Top with tomato wedges.
5. Blend cornstarch or tapioca starch with water or marinade juices if there is enough. Microwave 1-2 minutes until slightly thickened. Pour over meat and vegetables and heat 2-3 minutes.
6. Standing time 5 minutes. Serve on rice.

▤Pepper Steak

30 mL	2	Tablespoons cooking oil
454-681 g	1-1½	pounds round or sirloin steak, cut into strips
		Marinate steak 2-4 hours in:
30-60 mL	2-4	Tablespoons soy sauce
1 mL	¼	teaspoon ginger powder
1 mL	¼	teaspoon garlic powder
2	2	medium green peppers, cut into strips
250 mL	1	cup sliced onion
1 mL	¼	teaspoon salt
1 mL	¼	teaspoon pepper
15-30 mL	1-2	Tablespoons cornstarch or tapioca starch
125 mL	½	cup beef broth or 1 bouillon cube dissolved in ¾ cup hot water

1. Preheat browning dish with 2 Tablespoons (30 mL) oil for 4 minutes on *high*.
2. Cover and microwave beef strips 5-7 minutes on *high*, stirring once at 3 minutes.
3. Add green peppers, onions, salt and pepper to beef. Cover and microwave 5-6 minutes on *high*. Stir at 3 minutes.
4. Stir in cornstarch or tapioca starch, blended with beef broth.
5. Microwave 3-5 minutes on *high* or until sauce is thickened. Serve with rice.

Beef Stroganoff

781 g	1½	pounds round or sirloin steak strips
30-60 mL	2-4	Tablespoons white cooking wine, optional
30 mL	2	Tablespoons cooking oil
125 mL	½	cup chopped onions
284 mL	10	oz can sliced mushrooms, drained
1 mL	¼	teaspoon garlic powder
2 mL	½	teaspoon salt
1 mL	¼	teaspoon pepper
175 mL	1	bouillon cube, dissolved in ¾ cup hot water
30 mL	2	Tablespoons ketchup
1 mL	¼	teaspoon dry mustard
30 mL	2	Tablespoons flour
125-250 mL	½-1	cup sour cream

1. If using round steak, marinate strips in white wine.
2. Heat browning pan with 2 Tablespoons (30 mL) oil for 4 minutes on *high*.
3. Place steak and onions in browning pan. Cover and microwave 5 minutes on *high*. Stir once. Cook until meat loses its pink color.
4. Stir into meat: mushrooms, garlic powder, salt and pepper.
5. Mix bouillon cube and water, ketchup and dry mustard. Mix well and stir into meat. Cover and microwave 10 minutes on *high*. Stir once.
6. Mix flour and sour cream together to form a paste, then stir into meat. Microwave 2-4 minutes on *high*.
7. Standing time 5 minutes.

Tomato Soup Meat Loaf

681 g	1½	pounds hamburger
125 mL	½	cup bread crumbs
1	1	egg
125 mL	½	cup milk
50 mL	¼	cup chopped celery
50 mL	¼	cup onion, chopped finely
2 mL	½	teaspoon salt
1 mL	¼	teaspoon pepper
1 mL	¼	teaspoon sage powder
1 mL	¼	teaspoon garlic powder
0.5 mL	⅛	teaspoon paprika
284 mL	10	oz can tomato soup

1. Mix together hamburger, crumbs, egg, milk, celery, onion and seasoning. Mix all ingredients well.
2. Place a glass, open end down in the center of a 2 quart (2L) casserole dish. This takes place of a bundt pan.
3. Mold hamburger mixture around the glass.
4. Cover with plastic wrap and microwave 10 minutes on *high*. Drain extra fat from meatloaf.
5. Spread tomato soup on meatloaf. Cover and microwave 5-6 minutes on *high*.
6. Standing time 5 minutes.

Extra Tip

The open glass to casserole, absorbs extra hamburger grease.

≡Easy Hamburger Stroganoff

454 g	1	pound ground hamburger
284 mL	10	oz can sliced mushrooms
284 mL	10	oz can cream of mushroom soup
125 mL	½	cup chopped onion
2 mL	½	teaspoon salt
1 mL	¼	teaspoon pepper
1 mL	¼	teaspoon garlic powder
1 mL	¼	teaspoon dry mustard
30 mL	2	Tablespoons ketchup
250 mL	1	cup sour cream
15 mL	1	Tablespoon flour

1. Crumble hamburger into a 2-3 quart (2-3L) microproof casserole dish. Cover and microwave 4 minutes on *high*, or until meat loses pink color. Stir at 2 minutes.
2. Drain fat. Add remaining ingredients except sour cream and flour. Cover and microwave 6-8 minutes on *high*. Stir at 3-4 minutes.
3. Blend in sour cream and flour. Microwave 2-3 minutes on *high*.
4. Serve over cooked noodles.

Warming Buns — Microwave 6-8 buns in a wicker basket, 25-30 seconds on *high*. Buns heat from the inside out. Short heating time prevents buns from becoming dried out.

≡Burgundy Meat Balls

681 g	1½	pounds ground hamburger
125 mL	½	cup bread crumbs
50 mL	¼	cup chopped onions
1	1	egg beaten
50 mL	¼	cup milk
1 mL	¼	teaspoon garlic powder
2 mL	½	teaspoon salt
1 mL	¼	teaspoon pepper
30 mL	2	Tablespoons cooking oil
30 mL	2	Tablespoons flour
50 mL	¼	cup water
125 mL	½	cup red wine
		chopped parsley

1. Combine hamburger, bread crumbs, onion, egg, milk and dry seasoning. Mix and shape into small meatballs.
2. Preheat browning pan for 4 minutes on *high*, with 2 Tablespoons (30 mL) oil.
3. Cover and microwave meatballs 3 minutes on *high*. Turn meatballs and cook 3 minutes longer. Remove meatballs into a dish. Keep warm.
4. Stir flour, water and wine. Cook in browning dish and pan drippings for 3 minutes on *high*. Return meatballs to sauce. Cover and microwave 5 minutes. Sprinkle with chopped parsley and serve over noodles.

▤Porcupine Meatballs

908 g	2	pounds ground hamburger
250 mL	1	cup instant or quick cooking rice
2	2	eggs
50 mL	¼	cup chopped onions
2 mL	½	teaspoon salt
1 mL	¼	teaspoon pepper
1 mL	¼	teaspoon garlic powder
284 mL	10	oz can mushroom soup
5 mL	1	teaspoon parsley flakes

1. Mix hamburger, rice, eggs, onion, salt, pepper, garlic powder.
2. Shape into meatballs and arrange in a circle in a 9″ (23 cm) pie plate. Cover with wax paper. Microwave 4-5 minutes on *high*.
3. Drain fat and place meatballs into a 3 quart (3L) casserole dish.
4. Pour in mushroom soup and sprinkle with parsley flakes.
5. Cover and microwave 5 minutes on *high*, stir and microwave another 5 minutes.

 A Steaming Microwave — If condensation builds up on the walls and glass of the microwave; wipe off and check that the vents on the microwave are not obstructed.

Polynesian Meatballs

454 g	1	pound ground lean beef
50 mL	¼	cup crackers or bread crumbs
50 mL	¼	cup finely chopped onions
50 mL	¼	cup milk
1	1	egg
1 mL	¼	teaspoon salt
1 mL	¼	teaspoon pepper
		Pinch of garlic powder

1. Mix all ingredients together. Shape into 1 inch meat balls.
2. Microwave 3-4 minutes on *high* in a round microproof plate. Cover meatballs with wax paper.
3. Drain meatballs and place them in a deep casserole dish.

Sauce

125 mL	½	cup water
125 mL	½	cup reserved pineapple juice
30 mL	2	Tablespoons soy sauce
30 mL	2	Tablespoons vinegar
50 mL	¼	cup sugar
30 mL	2	Tablespoons cornstarch or tapioca powder
1	1	large green pepper, cut into small pieces
398 mL	14	oz can pineapple chunks or tidbits

1. Combine water, pineapple juice, soy sauce, vinegar, sugar and cornstarch or tapioca powder. Mix well in a 4 cup (1L) measuring pitcher.
2. Microwave green peppers for 3-4 minutes on *high*.
3. Microwave the sauce on *medium high* for 3-5 minutes. Stir the sauce twice before it is completely thickened.
4. Add green peppers and pineapple chunks to meatballs. Add the thickened sauce.
5. Microwave on *high* for 5 minutes. Stir the meatballs; cover and microwave another 5 minutes on *high*.

▤Left Over Hamburger Casserole

454 g	1	pound precooked hamburger
250 mL	1	cup diced celery
50 mL	¼	cup diced onions
375 mL	1½	cups diced cooked potatoes
250 mL	1	cup cooked carrots
500 mL	2	cups stewed tomatoes
2 mL	½	teaspoon salt
1 mL	¼	teaspoon pepper
50 mL	¼	cup cornflake crumbs

1. Cover and microwave hamburger, celery and onions, for 3-4 minutes on *high*, in a 2 quart (2L) casserole dish.
2. Drain fat and mix all ingredients together, except for the cornflakes. Place mixture into a 9" x 9" (2.5L) baking dish.
3. Cover with paper towel or wax paper and microwave 12-15 minutes on *medium*.
4. Sprinkle cornflakes on top of casserole during standing time.

▤Creamed Hamburger with Mushrooms

454 g	1	pound ground hamburger
284 mL	10	oz can mushrooms stems and pieces. Drain and reserve liquid
50 mL	¼	cup chopped onion
1 mL	¼	teaspoon pepper
2 mL	½	teaspoon salt
2	2	drops tabasco sauce
30 mL	2	Tablespoons flour
125 mL	½	cup milk
		English muffins, split and toasted
		grated Parmesan cheese
		parsley flakes

1. Crumble hamburger into 2 quart (2L) casserole dish. Cover and microwave 4 minutes on *high*. Stir and drain fat.
2. Add mushrooms, onions, pepper, salt, tabasco sauce. Cover and microwave 5 minutes on *high*.
3. Mix flour and milk into a paste. Pour over hamburger ingredients. Stir well and microwave 3 minutes on *high*. If you find the sauce is too thick, add ½ cup (125 mL) mushroom liquid into the hamburger. Mix well.
4. Serve on English muffins. Sprinkle lightly with Parmesan cheese and parsley flakes.

▤Hot Chile

908 g	2	pounds ground hamburger
1	1	large green pepper, chopped
25 mL	½	cup celery, chopped
250 mL	1	cup onion, chopped
796 mL	2-	28 oz cans kidney beans
284 mL	10	oz can sliced mushrooms
284 mL	10	oz can tomato soup
398 mL	14	oz can stewed tomatoes
30 mL	2	Tablespoons chile powder
1 mL	¼	teaspoon garlic powder
5 mL	1	teaspoon salt
2 mL	½	teaspoon pepper
2	2	drops tabasco sauce, optional

1. Crumble hamburger into a microwave simmer pot. Cover and micro-wave 4 minutes on *high*. Stir once at 2 minutes.
2. Drain fat from hamburger. Add all the ingredients. Stir well and cover simmer pot.
3. Cover and microwave 10 minutes on *high*. Stir once and microwave another 5-8 minutes on *medium*.
4. Standing time 5-8 minutes.

≣Quick Sloppy Joes

681 g	1½	pounds hamburger
250 mL	1	cup chopped onion
125 mL	½	cup chopped celery
125 mL	½	cup chopped green pepper
284 mL	10	oz can tomato sauce
15 mL	1	Tablespoon brown sugar
15 mL	1	Tablespoon vinegar
50 mL	3	Tablespoons chili powder
2 mL	½	teaspoon salt
1 mL	¼	teaspoon pepper
0.5 mL	⅛	teaspoon garlic powder
		Toasted hamburger buns

1. Crumble hamburger into a 2 quart (2L) microproof casserole dish. Cover and microwave for 4 minutes on *high*. Stir and drain fat.
2. Add onion, celery, green peppers, tomato sauce, brown sugar, vinegar and seasonings. Cover and microwave 6 minutes on *high*.
3. Microwave another 5 minutes on *high*, covered.
4. Standing time 5 minutes.
5. Spoon over toasted hamburger buns.

≡Microwave Lasagne

731 g	1½	pounds hamburger
170 g	6	oz can tomato paste
454 g	16	oz can stewed tomatoes
5 mL	1	teaspoon parsley flakes
2 mL	½	teaspoon garlic powder
2 mL	½	teaspoon salt
1 mL	¼	teaspoon pepper
8 mL	1½	teaspoons mixed Italian seasoning *or*
2 mL	½	teaspoon oregano
2 mL	½	teaspoon basil
2 mL	½	teaspoon thyme
375 mL	1½	cups creamed cottage cheese
125 mL	½	cup grated Parmesan cheese (divide in half)
8	8	precooked lasagne noodles
375 mL	1½	cups grated mozzarella cheese, or 6-8 mozzarella cheese slices

1. Crumble hamburger in a microwave simmer pot. Cover and microwave 5 minutes on *high*. Stir hamburger at 3 minutes. Drain fat before adding other ingredients.
2. Stir in tomato paste, stewed tomatoes and dry seasonings. Mix well. Cover and microwave 10 minutes on *medium* for seasonings to blend with sauce.
3. Stir together cottage cheese and ¼ cup (50 mL) parmesan cheese. Set aside.
4. In a microproof lasagne dish, alternate layers of noodles, meat sauce, mozzarella cheese and cottage cheese mixture. This makes two layers.
5. On top of last layer, put meat sauce and remaining parmesan cheese.
6. Cover and microwave 15-20 minutes on *medium* or until hot in centre.
7. Let stand 5-10 minutes, covered with shiny side of foil to lasagne.

Soft Taco Shell Mexi Casserole

4-6	4-6	soft taco shells
454 g	1	pound hamburger
125 mL	½	cup green pepper, chopped
125 mL	½	cup onion, chopped
1	1	envelope taco seasoning mix
284 mL	10	oz can tomato soup
284 mL	10	oz can tomato paste
125 mL	½	cup black olives, sliced
50 mL	¼	cup water
2 mL	½	teaspoon chili powder
250 mL	1	cup sour cream
2	2	eggs
1 mL	¼	teaspoon pepper
500 mL	2	cups broken corn chips
500 mL	2	cups shredded Chedder cheese

1. Place 2-3 soft taco shells into a 9" x 9" (2.5L) microproof dish.
2. Crumble hamburger into a 2 quart (2L) casserole dish. Add green pepper and onions. Cover and microwave 4-5 minutes on *high*. Stir and drain fat.
3. Mix in taco seasoning, tomato soup, tomato paste, olives, water and chili powder. Cover and microwave 10 minutes on *high*, until slightly thickened.
4. Blend sour cream, eggs and pepper together in small bowl.
5. Spoon half meat mixture on taco shells, followed by half sour cream mixture.
6. Repeat to make two layers.
7. Sprinkle corn chips and cheese over casserole. Cover and microwave 5-10 minutes on *medium* or until cheese has melted.
8. Standing time 5 minutes.

▤Stuffed Rolled Minute Steak

908 g	2	pounds minute steak, cut into rectangles
		Stuffing:
125 mL	½	cup chopped onion
50 mL	¼	cup chopped celery
30 mL	2	Tablespoons butter or margarine
250 mL	1	cup bread crumbs
1 mL	¼	teaspoon garlic powder
2 mL	½	teaspoon salt
1 mL	¼	teaspoon pepper
		Sprinkle of sage, thyme or oregano
1	1	egg
30 mL	2	Tablespoons water (optional)

Sauce

50 mL	¼	cup flour
30 mL	2	Tablespoons of onion soup mix
125 mL	½	cup water
5 mL	1	teaspoon Worcestershire sauce

1. Combine onion, celery and butter or margarine in a medium bowl. Microwave 3-4 minutes on *high*. Stir in bread crumbs, seasoning, water and beaten egg. Moisten bread crumbs well.
2. Spread equal amounts of stuffing over steak. Roll pieces and secure with tooth picks.
3. Blend flour, onion soup mix, Worcestershire sauce and water. Mix well. Microwave 2-3 minutes or until sauce is slightly thick, stirring once.
4. Arrange steak rolls in a 4 quart (4L) casserole dish. Spoon sauce over rolls. Cover with plastic wrap, vent. Microwave 20 minutes on *medium*.
5. Turn rolls over, spoon sauce over rolls. Re-cover and microwave 10-15 minutes or until meat is fork tender.
6. Standing time 10 minutes.

≡Swiss Round Steak Special

30 mL	2	Tablespoons cooking oil
454-908 g	1-2	pounds round steak, cut into serving sizes and pounded until steaks are ¼″ thick
454 g	16	oz can stewed tomatoes
1	1	envelope dry onion soup mix
1 mL	¼	teaspoon salt
1 mL	¼	teaspoon pepper
2 mL	½	teaspoon basil
30-50 mL	2-3	Tablespoons flour
125 mL	½	cup cold water
125 mL	½	cup shredded mozzarella cheese

1. Preheat browning dish with 2 Tablespoons (30 mL) oil for 4 minutes on *high*.
2. Cover and microwave steak pieces 8 minutes on *high*, turning meat at 4 minutes.
3. Combine stewed tomatoes, dry onion soup mix, salt, pepper and basil into a microwave simmer pot. Mix well and add meat. Cover and microwave 10 minutes on *high*. Stir at 5 minutes.
4. Mix flour and water, pour into meat mixture. Cover and microwave 10 minutes on *medium*, or until meat is tender.
5. Place shredded cheese on meat mixture during standing time. Cheese will melt slowly.
6. Standing time 5 minutes.

Swiss Steak and Mushroom Sauce

781 g	1½	pounds minute steak
15 mL	1	Tablespoon vinegar
30 mL	2	Tablespoons cooking oil
284 mL	10	oz can mushroom soup
2 mL	½	teaspoon kitchen bouquet
50 mL	3	Tablespoons flour
1 mL	¼	teaspoon dry mustard
2 mL	½	teaspoon salt
1 mL	¼	teaspoon pepper

1. Brush vinegar on steak pieces, and let marinate 15 minutes.
2. Preheat browning dish with 2 Tablespoons (30 mL) oil for 4 minutes on *high*.
3. Cover and microwave steak pieces for 8 minutes on *high*, turning meat at 4 minutes.
4. Combine mushroom soup, kitchen bouquet, flour, dry mustard, salt and pepper. Pour over steak.
5. Cover and microwave 15 minutes on *medium*, turning meat at 7 minutes.

≡Left Over Roast Beef Stew

750 mL	3	cups cubed roast beef
250 mL	1	cup chopped onion
250 mL	1	cup sliced carrots
250 mL	1	cup diced potatoes
125 mL	½	cup celery
2	2	beef bouillon cubes
30-50 mL	2-3	Tablespoons cornstarch or tapioca starch
5 mL	1	teaspoon salt
1 mL	¼	teaspoon pepper
1 mL	¼	teaspoon garlic powder

1. Cover and microwave beef and vegetables in a microwave simmer pot for 15 minutes on *high*. Stir ingredients twice.
2. Dissolve bouillon cubes in one cup (250 mL) water. Add cornstarch, salt, pepper and garlic powder, stirring until blended. Add this mixture to the meat and vegetables.
3. Microwave covered, for 15 minutes on *high*. Stir and microwave another 10 minutes on *medium*, or until vegetables are tender.
4. Standing time 5-8 minutes.

▤Bavarian Beef on Rice

30 mL	2	Tablespoons cooking oil
454 g	1	pound sirloin or round steak, cut into strips
3	3	sliced carrots
1	1	medium sliced onion
125 mL	½	cup beer
5 mL	1	teaspoon salt
1 mL	¼	teaspoon pepper
1 mL	¼	teaspoon garlic powder
10 mL	2	teaspoons brown sugar
5-10 mL	1-2	Tablespoons cornstarch or tapioca starch
125 mL	½	cup beef broth or 1 bouillon cube dissolved in hot water
2	2	drops tabasco sauce (optional)
750 mL	3	cups hot cooked rice

1. Heat browning pan with 2 Tablespoons (30 mL) oil for 4 minutes on *high*.
2. Cover and microwave steak strips 4 minutes on *high*. Stir.
3. Add carrots, onions, beer and dry ingredients. Cover and microwave 10 minutes on *high*. Stir at 5 minutes.
4. Mix cornstarch or tapioca starch with beef broth. Mix into meat ingredients. Cover and microwave 8-10 minutes on *high* or until carrots are cooked.
5. Standing time 5 minutes. Spoon over hot rice.

▓Oriental Liver with Vegetables

454 g	1	pound beef or pork liver, cut into bit size pieces
		Marinade:
30 mL	2	Tablespoons sesame seed oil
15 mL	1	Tablespoon soy sauce
15 mL	1	Tablespoon oyster sauce
5 mL	1	teaspoon sugar
5 mL	1	teaspoon ginger powder
125 mL	½	cup chopped onion
		Vegetables of your choice (celery, carrots, broccoli or Chinese vegetables)
30 mL	2	Tablespoons cornstarch or tapioca starch
125 mL	½	cup water

1. Marinate liver 2-3 hours.
2. Heat browning pan with 2 Tablespoons (30 mL) oil for 4 minutes on *high*.
3. Cover and microwave liver 4-5 minutes on *high*.
4. Add chopped onion and vegetables of your choice.
5. Cover and microwave liver and vegetables 10 minutes on *high*. Stir at 5 minutes.
6. Mix cornstarch or tapioca starch with water.
7. Add to liver mixture. Microwave 3-4 minutes on *high* or until sauce has thickened.

Poultry, Fish, Sauces and Marinades

Browning agents, melted butter and paprika, crumb mixtures and different sauces can be used to give poultry color for eye appeal.

Chicken and Cornish hens cook quickly and well in a microwave. Do not stuff poultry with bread dressing before cooking as the stuffing will taste metallic due to the absorption of the blood juices. The dressing can be cooked separately in a casserole dish.

Cooking fish in the microwave makes it moist, tender and delicious. It can be cooked in crumb mixtures, creamed or poached and stuffed. When cooked, the flesh should be opaque and flake easily with a fork. Standing time is minimal as fish cooks quickly. Be careful not to overcook your fish as it will become dry and rubbery.

More flour, cornstarch or tapioca starch should be added to thicken sauces and gravies. Moisture does not evaporate in microwave cooking as quickly as it does in conventional cooking. Stir sauces quickly (only two to three times) during cooking as stirring too often will slow down the cooking process.

From top to bottom
Honey Glazed Chicken Wings page 83.
Teriyaki Chicken Parts page 93.
Stuffed Salmon, Trout or White Fish page 101.

▤Roasting Poultry

1. Wash and dry poultry well.
2. Season with your favorite spices and seasonings, but do not salt your poultry until standing time. Use a browning agent to give a baked or roasted color to the meat.
3. Place poultry breast side up on a microwave meat rack, or on an inverted saucer. Place shiny side of foil to wing tips, drumstick ends and middle of breast; secure well with toothpicks.

Chicken

| 1.4 kg | 3 | pounds roasting chicken |

1. Microwave on *high* for 10 minutes. Turn chicken over and drain juices. Microwave for 6 minutes on *high*. Standing time is 2-4 minutes.

Cornish Hens

| 2-680 gm | 2 1½ | pound Cornish hens |

1. Microwave on *high* for 10 minutes. Turn hens over. Microwave on *high* for 6 minutes. Standing time is 4 minutes.

Turkey

| 5.5 kg | 12 | pound turkey |

1. Use the same steps as chicken and Cornish hens, but cook the turkey on *high* for 10-12 minutes per pound, if not using a meat probe or automatic sensor.
2. If using a meat probe, placed probe into the fleshy part of the meat (eg. breast). Microwave until the probe reaches 180-190°F.
3. Half-way through cooking time, turn turkey over, breast side up and drain the juices.
4. A 10-12 pound turkey takes approximately 1 hour and 15 minutes.
5. Standing time is 20-40 minutes. Cover with foil. Meat is very juicy and is nice for slicing.

▦Oriental Pineapple Chicken

30 mL	2	Tablespoons cooking oil
2	2	whole chicken breasts, cut into strips
2	2	carrots sliced thinly
250 mL	1	cup sliced celery
125 mL	½	cup sliced onion
398 mL	14	oz can unsweetened pineapple chunks (save juice)
65 mL	4	Tablespoons soy sauce
30 mL	2	Tablespoons cornstarch or tapioca starch
1 mL	¼	teaspoon salt

1. Heat browning pan with 2 Tablespoons (30 mL) oil for 4 minutes on *high*.
2. Cover and microwave chicken strips for 4 minutes on *high*. Stir, drain then add carrots, celery, onion and pineapple chunks. Cover and microwave for 6 minutes on *high*.
3. Combine pineapple juice, soy sauce, cornstarch or tapioca starch and salt. Pour over chicken and vegetables. Cover and microwave 4 minutes on *high* stirring once.
4. Standing time 2-5 minutes.
5. Serve with rice or Chinese noodles.

▨Honey Glazed Chicken Wings

1.35 kg	2½-3	pounds chicken wings
125 mL	½	cup honey
125 mL	½	cup dark soy sauce
1 mL	¼	teaspoon dry mustard
0.5 mL	⅛	teaspoon ginger powder
1 mL	¼	teaspoon garlic powder
15 mL	1	Tablespoon cornstarch or tapioca starch

1. Cut through each chicken wing at the joints. Discard wing tips. Wash remaining pieces thoroughly and pat dry.
2. Combine honey, soy sauce, mustard, ginger powder and garlic powder, into a mixing bowl, stirring well. Add wings and marinate 2-4 hours.
3. Arrange wing parts in a round microproof 9" (23 cm) baking dish. Place thicker ends toward edge of dish.
4. Cover with waxpaper and microwave 10 minutes on *high*.
5. Mix marinade and cornstarch or tapioca starch together.
6. Turn chicken wings, brush with marinade mixture. Cover and microwave 8-10 minutes on *high*.
7. Standing time 2-4 minutes.

 Soften Crystalized Honey — Remove lid from jar of honey, or put desired amount to be softened into a microproof vessel. Microwave 2-2½ minutes on *high*, or until clear. Stir every 30 seconds. Cool before using as it becomes very hot.

▤Chicken Cordon Bleu

8	8	boneless chicken breasts
8	8	thin slices of ham
250 mL	1	cup shredded Swiss or mozzarella cheese
125 mL	½	cup melted butter or margarine
500 mL	2	cups bread crumbs mixed with corn flake crumbs
1 mL	¼	teaspoon pepper
1 mL	¼	teaspoon paprika
		Sprinkle of salt
30 mL	2	Tablespoons cooking oil

1. Pound chicken breasts with a meat mallet to flatten ¼" (1 mL) thick.
2. Place 1 slice of ham on each piece of chicken, then sprinkle with cheese.
3. Roll up chicken, tucking in sides, then fasten with tooth picks.
4. Dip rolled chicken in melted butter or margarine. Coat with crumb mixture and sprinkle with seasonings.
5. Preheat browning pan with 2 Tablespoons (30 mL) oil for 4 minutes on *high*.
6. Place chicken rolls in browning pan. Cover and microwave 10 minutes on *high*.
7. Rearrange chicken rolls from middle to outside of browning pan. Microwave uncovered for 5 minutes on *high*. They will have a baked dry appearance when ready.

Serve With Bechamel Sauce

125 mL	½	cup chopped onion
50 mL	¼	cup butter or margarine
175 mL	¾	cup chicken broth
125 mL	½	cup half and half cream
125 mL	½	cup white wine
50 mL	3	Tablespoons flour
1 mL	¼	teaspoon nutmeg
		Sprinkle of salt and pepper

1. Microwave onion and butter or margarine for 3 minutes on *high*, in a 4 cup (1L) measuring pitcher.
2. Mix chicken broth, cream, white wine and flour. Add dry seasonings and mix well.
3. Microwave for 4 minutes on *high*. Stir at 2 minutes then microwave until thickened.
4. Pour over Chicken Cordon Bleu.

▤Parmesan Chicken

8	8	boneless chicken breasts
250 mL	1	cup bread crumbs mixed with corn flake crumbs
50 mL	¼	cup Parmesan cheese
1	1	egg beaten
30 mL	2	Tablespoons cooking oil
250 mL	1	cup shredded mozzarella cheese
284 mL	10	oz can tomato sauce
1 mL	¼	teaspoon poultry seasoning
1 mL	¼	teaspoon oregano

1. Pound chicken breasts with meat mallet to flatten to ¼ " (1 mL) thickness.
2. Mix crumbs and cheese in a plate. Dip chicken breasts in egg then into crumb mixture until chicken is well coated.
3. Preheat browning pan with 2 Tablespoons (30 mL) oil for 4 minutes on *high*.
4. Place chicken breasts into browning pan. Microwave uncovered for 6 minutes on *high*.
5. Turn chicken breasts over, sprinkle with mozzarella cheese and spoon tomato sauce and seasonings over chicken. Cover and microwave 6-8 minutes on *medium*.
6. Sprinkle with extra Parmesan cheese and microwave 1 minute to melt cheese.
7. Standing time 4 minutes.

▤Greek Lemon Chicken

30 mL	2	Tablespoons cooking oil
8	8	boneless chicken breasts
65 mL	4	Tablespoons butter
125 mL	½	cup chopped onion
2 mL	½	teaspoon oregano
2 mL	½	teaspoon tarragon or marjoram
1 mL	¼	teaspoon salt
1 mL	¼	teaspoon pepper
1 mL	¼	teaspoon garlic powder
50 mL	¼	cup lemon juice
1 mL	¼	teaspoon lemon rind
75 mL	⅓	cup white wine

1. Preheat browning pan with 2 Tablespoons (30 mL) oil for 4 minutes on *high*.
2. Sear chicken breasts. Dot with butter and mix together all other ingredients. Pour over chicken breasts.
3. Cover and microwave 10 minutes on *high*. Rearrange chicken breasts and microwave 8 minutes on *high*.

Sauce For Chicken Breasts

125 mL	½	cup whipping cream
30 mL	2	Tablespoons cornstarch or tapioca starch
50 mL	¼	cup water
1 mL	¼	teaspoon salt
1 mL	¼	teaspoon pepper

1. Remove chicken from browning dish and mix cream into chicken drippings.
2. Microwave 2 minutes on *high*. Mix together cornstarch, water, salt and pepper and stir into cream mixture. Microwave 2 minutes on *high* and pour over chicken breasts.
3. Sprinkle with parsley flakes.
4. Serve over noodles or rice.

≡Chicken Provençale

6	6	slices chopped bacon
250 mL	1	cup chopped onion
2	2	carrots sliced thin
30 mL	2	Tablespoons cooking oil
1.35 kg	2½-3	pounds cut up chicken
50 mL	¼	cup brandy
2	2	medium chopped tomatoes
125 mL	½	cup red wine
1 mL	¼	teaspoon marjoram
1 mL	¼	teaspoon basil
2 mL	½	teaspoon parsley
1 mL	¼	teaspoon salt
1 mL	¼	teaspoon pepper
30 mL	2	Tablespoons flour
125 mL	½	cup cold water
5 mL	1	teaspoon kitchen bouquet

1. Microwave bacon, onions and carrots in a microproof bowl; 4 minutes on *high*. Stir at 2 minutes.
2. Preheat browning pan with 2 Tablespoons (30 mL) oil. Place thicker chicken parts to edge of browning dish. Cover and microwave 10 minutes on *high*.
3. Heat brandy in a 1 cup (250 mL) glass measuring pitcher for 15 seconds. Pour brandy over chicken parts and flame.
4. When flame goes out, put chicken into a simmer pot, and add all other ingredients except flour, water, and kitchen bouquet.
5. Cover and microwave 15 minutes on *medium*. Turn chicken parts over and microwave 10 minutes on *medium*.
6. Blend flour, water and kitchen bouquet until pasty, then add to chicken. Microwave 5 minutes.
7. Standing time 5 minutes.

≡Chicken Breasts with Pilaf

30 mL	2	Tablespoons cooking oil
4	4	chicken breasts, halved
1 mL	¼	teaspoon thyme
2 mL	½	teaspoon tarragon
1 mL	¼	teaspoon poultry seasoning
1 mL	¼	teaspoon salt
1 mL	¼	teaspoon pepper
Sprinkle		Sprinkle of paprika
30 mL	2	Tablespoons flour
250 mL	1	cup chicken broth

1. Preheat browning dish with 2 Tablespoons (30 mL) oil for 4 minutes on *high*.
2. Cover and sear chicken breasts in browning pan.
3. Sprinkle seasonings on chicken breasts. Cover and microwave 10 minutes on *high*.
4. Remove chicken breasts from browning pan and blend flour into drippings. Add chicken broth gradually. Microwave for 4 minutes on *high* or until mixture thickens. Put chicken breasts into sauce.

Pilaf

250 mL	1	cup rice
500 mL	2	cups hot water
2	2	chicken bouillon cubes
2 mL	½	teaspoon salt
15 mL	1	Tablespoon butter or margarine
284 mL	10	ounce can sliced mushrooms
125 mL	½	cup chopped celery
125 mL	½	cup slivered almonds

1. Combine all ingredients into a microproof 3 quart (3L) casserole dish or simmer pot.
2. Cover and microwave 6 minutes on *medium high*.
3. Stir rice ingredients, cover and microwave 6 minutes on *high*.
4. Standing time 5 minutes.
5. Reheat chicken breasts and sauce. Mound rice mixture in centre of plate. Surround with chicken breasts and spoon sauce over top.
6. Garnish with frosted grapes.

Frosted Grapes

		white seedless grape clusters
1	1	beaten egg white
125 mL	½	cup sugar

1. Dip grape clusters into egg white and roll in sugar.
2. Shake off excess.

≡Chicken Chow Microwave

250 mL	1	cup chopped celery
125 mL	½	cup chopped onion
500 mL	2	cups diced, cooked or canned chicken
398 mL	14	oz can pineapple tidbits, drained
284 mL	10	oz can mushroom soup
30 mL	2	Tablespoons soy sauce
1 mL	¼	teaspoon salt
0.5 mL	⅛	teaspoon pepper
113.4 g	14	oz can chow mein noodles

1. Microwave celery and onion in a microproof dish, for 4 minutes on *high*. Stir at 2 minutes.
2. Combine chicken, pineapple, mushroom soup and seasoning. Mix well.
3. Stir in 1 cup (250 mL) noodles. Pour ingredients into a 9″ x 9″ (2.5L) square or 9″ (23 cm) round microproof baking dish.
4. Sprinkle remaining noodles on top. Cover with paper towel and microwave 15-20 minutes on *medium*.
5. Standing time 5 minutes.

Coq Au Vin or Chicken in Wine

1.35 kg	2½-3	pounds cut up chicken
6	6	slices chopped bacon
250 mL	1	cup chopped onions
250 mL	1	cup sliced fresh mushrooms
125 mL	½	cup chicken broth
125 mL	½	cup red wine
1 mL	¼	teaspoon thyme
1 mL	¼	teaspoon garlic powder
1 mL	¼	teaspoon salt
1 mL	¼	teaspoon pepper
2 mL	½	teaspoon parsley flakes
30-50 mL	2-3	Tablespoons cornstarch or tapioca starch

1. Arrange thicker chicken parts to the outside edges of browning pan. Cover with lid and microwave 10 minutes on *high*. Drain chicken.
2. Microwave bacon and onion in a microproof bowl for 4-5 minutes on *high*. Stir at 2-3 minutes.
3. Add mushrooms, cooked onions and bacon to chicken parts.
4. Combine chicken broth, red wine, seasonings and cornstarch or tapioca starch. Stir well.
5. Pour mixture over chicken. Cover with lid and microwave 10 minutes on *medium*. Turn chicken over, cover and microwave 6-8 minutes on *medium*.
6. Standing time 5 minutes.

▓Chicken Curry

50 mL	¼	cup chopped onion
50 mL	¼	cup chopped celery
1.35 kg	2½-3	lb. cut up chicken
50 mL	¼	cup milk
75 mL	⅓	cup water
2 mL	½	teaspoon salt
1 mL	¼	teaspoon pepper
0.5 mL	⅛	teaspoon garlic powder
1 mL	¼	teaspoon sugar
30 mL	2	Tablespoons curry powder, or to taste
30 mL	2	Tablespoons cornstarch or tapioca starch
1	1	medium chopped tomato

Condiments: Shredded coconut, sliced green onions, seedless raisins, peanuts, chopped apple, Indian chutney. (See page 92).

1. Microwave onions and celery in a microproof dish for 4 minutes on *high*. Stir at 2 minutes.
2. Arrange thicker chicken parts to the outside edges of browning pan. Cover with lid and microwave 10 minutes on *high* Drain and turn chicken over.
3. Combine milk, water, salt, pepper, garlic powder, sugar, curry powder and cornstarch or tapioca starch. Mix well, add chopped tomato and pour over chicken.
4. Cover with lid and microwave 10 minutes on *medium*. Stir and turn chicken over. Add your favorite condiment. Cover and microwave 10 minutes on *medium*.
5. Standing time 5 minutes.

▤Indian Chutney

2	2	apples, chopped
125 mL	½	cup raisins
30 mL	2	Tablespoons chopped candied citrus fruit
50 mL	¼	cup brown sugar
75 mL	⅓	cup vinegar
50 mL	¼	cup water
5 mL	1	teaspoon curry powder
1 mL	¼	teaspoon salt
1 mL	¼	teaspoon ginger
1 mL	¼	teaspoon garlic powder
0.5 mL	⅛	teaspoon cloves
0.5 mL	⅛	teaspoon cinnamon

1. Combine ingredients into a microwave simmer pot. Cover and micro-wave 4 minutes on *high*. Stir, cover and microwave 4-6 minutes on *medium*.
2. Chill. Makes 1¾ cups (450 mL).

▤Teriyaki Chicken Parts

125 mL	½	cup soy sauce
50 mL	¼	cup white cooking wine
30 mL	2	Tablespoons brown sugar or
50 mL	¼	cup honey
1 mL	¼	teaspoon dry mustard
1 mL	¼	teaspoon ginger powder
30 mL	2	Tablespoons cornstarch or tapioca starch
		Sprinkle of garlic powder
1.35 kg	2½-3	pounds chicken parts

1. Combine soy sauce, wine, brown sugar or honey, mustard, ginger powder, garlic powder and cornstarch or tapioca starch. Mix well and microwave 2-3 minutes on *high*, stirring at 2 minutes. Microwave until slightly thickened.
2. Arrange thicker chicken parts to the outside edges of browning pan. Pour sauce on chicken. Cover with lid and microwave 10 minutes on *high*. Turn chicken over, cover and microwave 8-10 minutes on *high*.
3. Standing time 5 minutes.

Quick Fruit Sauce or Glaze — Place desired amount of jam or jelly in a microproof measuring pitcher. Microwave on *high* 1-2 minutes uncovered. Use for dessert topping, sauce or meat glaze.

▤Ukrainian Style Cream Chicken

1.35 kg	2½-3	pounds cut up chicken
1	1	bay leaf
250 mL	1	cup hot water
5 mL	1	teaspoon salt
1 mL	¼	teaspoon pepper
1 mL	¼	teaspoon garlic powder
500 mL	2	cups whipping cream
15 mL	1	Tablespoon flour
5 mL	1	teaspoon dill

1. Place chicken parts in a microproof simmer pot. Add bay leaf, water and salt. Cover and microwave 10 minutes on *high*.
2. Combine pepper, garlic powder, whipping cream, flour and dill. Mix until cream is slightly thickened. Pour over drained chicken. Cover and microwave 10-12 minutes on *medium*. Stir chicken and sauce at 6 minutes.
3. If cream mixture is too thick add ¼ cup (50 mL) chicken stock.
4. Standing time 5 minutes.

▤Barbecued Chicken

1.35 kg	2½-3	pounds cut up chicken
175 mL	¾	cup barbecue sauce, home made or purchased sauce
1 mL	¼	teaspoon garlic powder
2 mL	½	Tablespoon parsley flakes

1. Arrange chicken parts in a browning pan, thicker pieces toward outside of dish.
2. Brush half the sauce over chicken and sprinkle with ½ of the garlic powder and parsley flakes.
3. Cover with paper towel and microwave 10 minutes on *high*.
4. Turn chicken over, brush with remaining sauce and seasonings. Cover and microwave 10 minutes on *high*.
5. Standing time 5 minutes.

▤Onion Soup Baked Chicken

1.35 kg	2½-3	pounds cut up chicken
125 mL	½	cup melted butter of margarine
1	1	package dry onion soup mix

1. Dip chicken in butter or margarine and in soup mix.
2. Arrange chicken parts in a browning pan, thicker pieces toward outside of the dish.
3. Cover with lid and microwave 10 minutes on *high*. Turn chicken over. Cover and microwave 8-10 minutes on *high*.
4. Standing time 5 minutes.

▤Golden Mushroom Soup Chicken

284 mL	10	oz can golden mushroom soup
284 mL	10	oz can sliced mushrooms
5 mL	1	teaspoon basil
2 mL	½	teaspoon salt
1 mL	¼	teaspoon pepper
1 mL	¼	teaspoon parsley flakes
1 mL	¼	teaspoon garlic powder
1.35 kg	2½-3	pounds cut up chicken

1. Combine mushroom soup, mushrooms and seasonings. Mix well to blend.
2. Arrange thicker chicken parts to the outside edges of browning pan. Spoon sauce over chicken.
3. Cover with lid and microwave 10 minutes on *high*. Turn chicken over, cover and microwave 8-10 minutes on *high*.
4. Standing time 5 minutes.

▤Mushroom Soup Smothered Chicken

1.35 kg	2½-3	pounds cut up chicken
5 mL	1	teaspoon kitchen bouquet
284 mL	10	oz can cream of mushroom soup
284 mL	10	oz can sliced mushrooms, drained
1 mL	¼	teaspoon salt
1 mL	¼	teaspoon pepper
		Sprinkle of garlic powder

1. Arrange chicken parts in a browning pan, thicker pieces toward outside of dish.
2. Cover with lid and microwave 10 minutes on *high*.
3. Turn chicken parts over and mix kitchen bouquet into mushroom soup; pour over chicken. Place sliced mushrooms and seasonings over chicken.
4. Cover and microwave 10 minutes on *high*. Stir sauce at 5 minutes.
5. Standing time 5 minutes.

Shake and Bake Chicken

1.35 kg	2½-3	pounds cut up chicken
125 mL	½	cup milk
1	1	package shake and bake coating mix

1. Dip chicken in milk and into shake and bake mix
2. Arrange chicken parts in a browning pan, thicker pieces towards outside of dish.
3. Cover with paper towel and microwave 10 minutes on *high*. Turn chicken over. Cover and microwave 8-10 minutes on *high*.
4. Standing time 5 minutes.

Cornish Hens with Honey Marmalade Glaze

2	2	Cornish hens, split in half
0.5 mL	⅛	teaspoon ginger
2 mL	½	teaspoon paprika
65 mL	4	Tablespoons liquid honey
175 mL	¾	cup mixed marmalade jam

1. Place cornish hens, thicker parts, to outside of browning pan. Sprinkle with ginger and paprika.
2. Cover with lid and microwave 10 minutes on *high*.
3. Drain chicken juices and turn cornish hens over.
4. Mix honey and jam together in a 1 cup (250 mL) measuring cup. Microwave 2 minutes on *high* and stir.
5. Brush glaze on cornish hens. Cover and microwave 8 minutes.
6. Turn cornish hens over, brush on glaze. Uncover and microwave 3-4 minutes. Brush on remaining glaze.
7. Standing time 5 minutes.

▤Chicken Stew and Dumplings

1.35 kg	2½-3	pounds cut up chicken
50 mL	¼	cup water
125 mL	½	cup chopped celery
125 mL	½	cup chopped onion
500 mL	2	cups sliced carrots
1	1	bay leaf
2 mL	½	teaspoon salt
1 mL	¼	teaspoon pepper
		sprinkle of garlic powder
284 mL	10	oz can cream of chicken soup

1. Place chicken in a microproof simmer pot with water, celery, onion, carrots, bay leaf and dry seasonings.
2. Cover and microwave 15 minutes on *medium*.
3. Stir chicken and vegetables. Add cream of chicken soup. Cover and microwave 15-20 minutes on *medium* or until chicken and vegetables are tender.

Dumplings

375 mL	1½	cups flour
2 mL	½	teaspoon parsley flakes
10 mL	2	teaspoons baking powder
1 mL	¼	teaspoon salt
150 mL	⅔	cup milk
30 mL	2	Tablespoons oil
1	1	egg beaten

1. Combine dry ingredients with the liquids. Stir with fork until flour is moistened.
2. Spoon dumplings on top of stew.
3. Cover and microwave 5-6 minutes on *medium high* or until puffy and not doughy.

≡Creamed Left Over Turkey

15 mL	1	Tablespoon butter or margarine
125 mL	½	cup chopped onion
500 mL	2	cups diced cooked turkey
500 mL	2	cups frozen peas
125 mL	½	leftover turkey gravy
1 mL	¼	teaspoon nutmeg
2 mL	½	teaspoon salt
1 mL	¼	teaspoon pepper
1 mL	¼	teaspoon parsley flakes

1. In a 2½ quart (2.5L) microproof casserole dish, microwave butter or margarine and onion for 3 minutes on *high*, stirring at 2 minutes.
2. Stir in turkey, peas, gravy and seasonings.
3. Cover and microwave 8-10 minutes on *medium*, stirring at 4 minutes.

Cream Sauce

20 mL	1½	Tablespoons butter or margarine
20 mL	1½	Tablespoons flour
250 mL	1	cup milk or half and half cream
2	2	eggs beaten
1 mL	¼	teaspoon salt

1. In a 4 cup (1L) measuring pitcher, melt butter or margarine. Mix in flour and slowly add milk, stirring well. Add beaten eggs, stir and microwave 3 minutes on *medium*, stirring at 2 minutes. Cook until thickened.
2. Pour sauce over turkey and stir well.
3. Serve over rice or buttered noodles.

▤Baked Salmon Steaks

125 mL	½	cup chopped celery
50 mL	¼	cup butter or margarine
2 mL	½	teaspoon parsley flakes
1 mL	¼	teaspoon salt
2 mL	½	teaspoon dill weed
1 mL	¼	teaspoon pepper
50 mL	¼	cup white cooking wine
4	4	salmon steaks
		Sprinkle of paprika

1. Combine celery, butter, parsley flakes, salt, dill and pepper in a 2 cup (500 mL) measuring pitcher.
2. Microwave 3-4 minutes on *high* or until celery is tender. Stir in wine.
3. Arrange salmon in an oblong baking dish, and spoon butter/wine mixture over salmon. Sprinkle paprika.
4. Cover with paper towel or wax paper and microwave 5-6 minutes on *high*.
5. Salmon will flake when cooked.
6. Standing time 3 minutes.

 Drying Chives — Cut chives into small pieces. Place between paper towels. Microwave 2-4 minutes on *high*.

≡Stuffed Salmon, Trout or White Fish

900-1300 g	2-3	pounds your choice of fish
50 mL	¼	cup butter or margarine
50 mL	¼	cup chopped onion
50 mL	¼	cup chopped celery
250 mL	1	cup bread crumbs
1	1	egg beaten
15 mL	1	Tablespoon parsley flakes
30 mL	2	Tablespoons water
30 mL	2	Tablespoons lemon juice
2 mL	½	teaspoon salt
1 mL	¼	teaspoon pepper
1 mL	¼	teaspoon sage powder
		Sprinkle of paprika

1. Wash fish in cold water and pat dry.
2. Combine butter or margarine, onion and celery in a 2 quart (2L) glass bowl. Cover and microwave 2-3 minutes on *high*.
3. Add all other ingredients and mix well or until bread crumbs are completely moistened.
4. Stuff salmon with mixture and place on microproof oval dish. Brush salmon with melted butter or margarine. Sprinkle with paprika.
5. Shield head and tail with foil shiny side up. Cover with plastic wrap and vent. Microwave 10-12 minutes on *high* or until fish flakes easily with a fork.
6. Remove foil and microwave 2 minutes on *high* uncovered.
7. Standing time 2-4 minutes.
8. Place a slice of pimiento stuffed olive in the eye cavity.

Optional

A mixture of crab meat and shrimp can be added to bread crumb stuffing.

▤Poached Fish with Almonds

30 mL	2	Tablespoons cooking oil
150 mL	⅔	cup slivered or sliced almonds
50 mL	¼	cup butter or margarine
50 mL	¼	cup lemon juice
50 mL	¼	cup white cooking wine
2 mL	½	teaspoon dill weed or seed
1 mL	¼	teaspoon salt
1 mL	¼	teaspoon pepper
454-908 g	1-2	pounds fish fillets (white fish, sole, perch or haddock)

1. Preheat browning dish with 2 Tablespoons (30 mL) oil for 4 minutes on *high*.
2. Combine almonds and butter or margarine. Microwave uncovered 3-4 minutes on *high*, until almonds are golden brown.
3. Stir in lemon juice, wine, dill, salt and pepper. Arrange fish fillets in butter with thickest parts to the outside of browning dish.
4. Spoon sauce over fish. Cover and microwave 6-8 minutes on *high*.
5. Standing time 2 minutes.
6. Garnish with lemon slices or parsley.

Citrus Fruits — Microwave fruit 30 seconds on *high* before squeezing, to get more juice from the fruit. Roll fruit between your hands, cut and squeeze out the juices.

Sole with Lemon Parsley Butter

50 mL	3	Tablespoons lemon juice
125 mL	½	cup butter or margarine, melted
30 mL	2	Tablespoons cornstarch or tapioca starch
2 mL	½	teaspoon parsley flakes
0.5 mL	⅛	teaspoon celery salt
1 mL	¼	teaspoon salt
		dash of pepper
908 g	2	pounds thawed sole fillets

1. Blend lemon juice, butter or margarine, cornstarch or tapioca starch, parsley flakes, celery salt, salt and pepper. Mix well.
2. Dip each fillet into seasoned butter. Arrange fillets in a microproof round 9″ (23 cm) baking dish, with thick edges toward the outside of dish.
3. Cover with wax paper and microwave 6-8 minutes, or until fillets flake easily.
4. Standing time 5 minutes, covered.

Easy Shrimp or Scallop Curry

50 mL	¼	cup butter or margarine
125 mL	½	cup chopped onion
125 mL	½	cup chopped celery
50 mL	¼	cup chopped green pepper
125 mL	½	cup water
125 mL	½	cup milk
5 mL	1	teaspoon dry instant chicken bouillon
50 mL	3	Tablespoons flour
15 mL	1	tablespoon curry powder
454 g	16	oz. package frozen shrimp or scallops, thawed

1. Combine butter or margarine, onion, celery and peppers in a 2 quart (2L) glass casserole dish. Cover and microwave 3-4 minutes on *high*.
2. Mix together water, milk, chicken bouillon, flour and curry powder. Microwave 2-3 minutes on high. Add shrimp and sauce to vegetables.
3. Cover and microwave 10-12 minutes on *high*.
4. Serve on hot rice.

≣Tuna Cashew Casserole

113.4 g	4	oz can chow mein noodles
1-2	1-2	cans chunky tuna
284 mL	10	oz can mushroom soup
50 mL	¼	cup minced onion
125 mL	½	cup broken cashew nuts
1 mL	¼	teaspoon parsley flakes
1 mL	¼	teaspoon salt
1 mL	¼	teaspoon pepper

1. Set aside ½ cup (125 mL) chow mein noodles.
2. Combine and mix tuna, mushroom soup, onion, chow mein noodles, cashew nuts, parsley flakes, salt and pepper into a 3 quart (3L) casserole dish.
3. Cover and microwave 8-10 minutes on *medium*.
4. Sprinkle remaining crushed noodles on casserole during standing time of 2-4 minutes.

Cheese Toppings — Add cheese toppings during the last 1 or 2 minutes of cooking. Cheese will overcook if added sooner.

▤Microwave Salmon Loaf

397 g	14	ounce can of salmon
15 mL	1	Tablespoon chopped onion
30 mL	2	Tablespoons chopped celery
2	2	eggs
5 mL	1	teaspoon lemon juice
5 mL	1	teaspoon Worcestershire sauce
2 mL	½	teaspoon salt
1 mL	¼	teaspoon pepper
250 mL	1	cup milk
30 mL	2	Tablespoons melted butter or margarine
125 mL	½	cup bread crumbs

1. Drain salmon and mash, discarding bones and skin.
2. Add onion, celery, eggs, lemon juice, Worcestershire sauce, salt and pepper.
3. Combine milk, melted butter or margarine and bread crumbs. Mix until crumbs are completely moistened. Add to salmon mixture and mix well.
4. Place a juice glass in the middle of an 8" (20 cm) round microproof baking dish. Pour mixture around glass in baking dish.
5. Cover with wax paper and microwave 6-8 minutes on *medium*.

Extra Tip

(a) Serve salmon loaf with a mushroom soup, white or cheese sauce.
(b) The centre of the ring can be filled with creamed peas or other vegetables, before serving.

≡Salmon Creole Casserole

500 mL	2	cups cooked rice
1	1	egg
125 mL	½	cup diced celery
125 mL	½	cup diced onion
250 mL	1	cup frozen peas
198.4 g	7	oz can salmon
250 mL	1	cup canned tomatoes
5 mL	1	teaspoon lemon juice
5 mL	1	teaspoon chili powder
2 mL	½	teaspoon sugar
1 mL	¼	teaspoon salt
1 mL	¼	teaspoon pepper
15-30 mL	1-2	Tablespoons flour

1. Combine rice and beaten egg and line the bottom of a microproof 3 quart (3L) casserole dish. Save enough to cover top.
2. In a small bowl cover and microwave celery, onion and peas, for 5 minutes on *high*, stirring once.
3. Mix salmon, tomatoes, lemon juice, chili powder, sugar, salt, pepper and flour. Stir well. Add to celery, onion and pea ingredients.
4. Pour into rice lined baking dish. Top with remaining rice.
5. Cover with plastic wrap and microwave 10-15 minutes on *medium*.

Drying Lemon or Orange Peel — Place grated lemon or orange peel in a small microproof bowl. Microwave 1-2 minutes on *medium*.

▤Hollandaise Sauce

50 mL	¼	cup butter
2	2	egg yolks, beaten
10 mL	2	teaspoons lemon juice
50 mL	¼	cup half and half cream
1 mL	¼	teaspoon dry mustard
0.5 mL	⅛	teaspoon salt

1. Melt butter in a 2 cup (500 mL) measuring pitcher for 30 seconds on *high*.
2. Beat egg yolks, lemon juice, half and half cream, dry mustard and salt.
3. Microwave 2 minutes on *high* uncovered, stirring after 1 minute. Stir again at 30 seconds until sauce thickens slightly.
4. Makes ½ cup (125 mL).

▤Barbecue Sauce

250 mL	1	cup tomato juice
50 mL	¼	cup vinegar
50 mL	¼	cup catsup
5 mL	1	teaspoon Worcestershire sauce
30 mL	2	Tablespoons brown sugar
2 mL	½	teaspoon paprika
2 mL	½	teaspoon dry mustard
2 mL	½	teaspoon garlic powder
2 mL	½	teaspoon pepper
2 drops	2	drops liquid smoke (optional)
2 drops	2	drops of tabasco sauce
15-30 mL	1-2	Tablespoons cornstarch or tapioca starch

1. Combine all ingredients in a microproof simmer pot. Mix well.
2. Cover and microwave for 5-6 minutes on *medium high*, stirring twice, to dissolve the brown sugar.
3. Makes 2 cups (500 mL).

▤Everyday Basic White Sauce

30 mL	2	Tablespoons butter or margarine
30 mL	2	Tablespoons flour
2 mL	½	teaspoon salt
250 mL	1	cup milk

1. Melt butter in a 2 cup (500 mL) measuring pitcher, for 30 seconds on *medium high*.
2. Stir flour and salt into the liquid margarine or butter.
3. Gradually add milk, stirring until smooth.
4. Cook uncovered 3-4 minutes on *medium high*, until sauce is thickened. Stir sauce at least 2 times.
5. Makes 1 cup (250 mL).

Extra White Sauce Suggestions

Cheese Sauce — add ½-¾ cup (125-175 mL) grated Cheddar cheese Microwave 1 minute to melt cheese.
Stir once at 30 seconds

Dill Sauce — add 1-2 teaspoons (5-10 mL) dillweed and 1 teaspoon (5 mL) lemon juice to the hot sauce. Stir well.

▤Quick Sweet and Sour Sauce

398 mL	14	oz can crushed pineapple (drained)
175 mL		water added to pineapple juice to make ¾ cup
50 mL	¼	cup vinegar
50 mL	¼	cup brown sugar
15 mL	1	Tablespoon soy sauce
15-30 mL	1-2	Tablespoons cornstarch or tapioca starch

1. In a 4 cup (1L) measuring pitcher, add water, pineapple liquid, vinegar, brown sugar, soy sauce with corn starch. Stir well.
2. Microwave 2-3 minutes on *high* uncovered, stirring two times.
3. When sauce is thickened, add crushed pineapple. Stir well.
4. Microwave 1-2 minutes on *high*.

Extra Tip

If you like a red sauce instead of a brownish color, add 2 Tablespoons (30 mL) catsup.

▤Pork and Beef Marinades

Soy Marinade (oriental)

125 mL	½	cup soy sauce
30 mL	2	Tablespoons Worcestershire sauce
30 mL	2	Tablespoons lemon juice
1 mL	¼	teaspoon pepper
1 mL	¼	teaspoon ginger powder
1 mL	¼	teaspoon garlic powder

1. Mix all ingredients together and pour over meat.
2. Marinate 2-4 hours.

Beer Marinade

1	1	bottle of beer
1	1	medium onion, chopped
30 mL	2	Tablespoons Worcestershire sauce
1	1	bay leaf crumbled
2 mL	½	teaspoon salt
1 mL	¼	teaspoon pepper
1 mL	¼	teaspoon tarragon leaves
1 mL	¼	teaspoon garlic powder

1. Mix all ingredients together and pour over meat.
2. Marinate 2-4 hours.

Red or White Wine Marinade

250 mL	1	cup cooking wine (red or white)
125 mL	½	cup water
30 mL	2	Tablespoons parsley flakes
10 mL	2	teaspoons oregano
10 mL	2	teaspoons basil
2 mL	½	teaspoon salt
1 mL	¼	teaspoon thyme

1. Mix all ingredients together and pour over meat.
2. Marinate 2-4 hours.

Hawaiian Marinade

125 mL	½	cup pineapple juice
83 mL	⅓	cup cooking oil
50 mL	¼	cup soy sauce
15 mL	1	Tablespoon lemon juice
5 mL	1	teaspoon dry mustard
2 mL	½	teaspoon ginger powder
0.5 mL	⅛	teaspoon mace powder
50 mL	¼	cup brown sugar
50 mL	3	Tablespoons honey

1. Mix all ingredients together in a microproof 4 cup (1L) measuring pitcher.
2. Microwave 2 minutes on *high* to dissolve sugar and honey.
3. Cool and pour over meat.
4. Marinate 2-4 hours.

▤Gravy for Meats

30 mL	2	Tablespoons butter or margarine
60 mL	4	Tablespoons beef, pork, or poultry drippings
250 mL	1	cup beef, pork, or poultry juice or cold water
30 mL	2	Tablespoons flour
2 mL	½	teaspoon salt
1 mL	¼	teaspoon pepper
1 mL	¼	teaspoon garlic powder
2 mL	½	teaspoon kitchen bouquet (optional)

1. Combine butter or margarine and meat drippings into a 4 cup (1L) measuring cup. Microwave uncovered 1½-2 minutes until butter or margarine is melted.
2. Mix meat juices or cold water, flour, salt, pepper, garlic powder, and kitchen bouquet. Stir until flour is blended with liquid.
3. Microwave 3 minutes on *high*. Stir and microwave 2 minutes or until gravy is slightly thickened.

 Drying Herbs — Place parsley, celery leaves, mint leaves and herbs between sheets of paper towels. Microwave for 3-4 minutes on *medium*. Cool and crumble.

Desserts

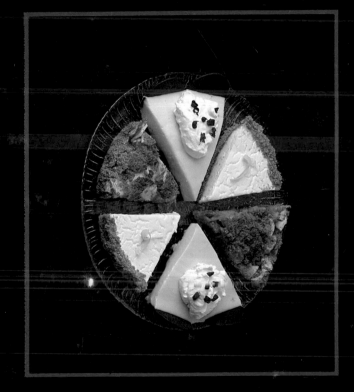

In converting your favorite quick bread recipe, reduce the amount of leavening agents (baking powder and soda) by ⅓ the normal amount. There will be a bitter after taste if too much leavening agent is used.

If a recipe contains sour cream or buttermilk, do not change the amount of soda used as it counteracts the sour taste of the baked bread.

In using a regular prepared cake mix, let the batter sit for 10 minutes before cooking. This will decrease the gases in the cake batter as the leavening agent can not be reduced.

When baking white cup cakes, use cinnamon, brown sugar, nut toppings, toasted coconut, food coloring, graham cracker crumbs and chocolate to eliminate a pale looking cup cake.

To enhance a pie crust appearance, use yellow food coloring, cocoa, egg yolk brushed over top, or caramelized microwave baste.

If the center of the cake is too moist after the right amount of baking time, elevate the cake plate on a saucer, fruit nappy or microproof rack to enable the microwave molecules to reach the centre of the cake.

from the top in a clockwise direction

114

▤Rice Pudding

3	3	eggs, beaten
500 mL	2	cups milk
125 mL	½	cup sugar
5 mL	1	teaspoon vanilla
500 mL	2	cups cooked rice
125 mL	½	cup precooked raisins
3 mL	½	teaspoon cinnamon
2 mL	¼	teaspoon nutmeg
250 mL	1	cup half and half cream

1. Combine eggs, milk, sugar and vanilla into a 2 quart (2L) microproof casserole dish. Mix well.
2. Add rice and raisins into mixture. Cover and microwave for 3 minutes on *medium* and stir. Sprinkle on cinnamon and nutmeg. Cover and microwave 5 minutes on *medium*. Stir at 3 minutes. Microwave until rice is thickened.
3. Standing time 30 minutes without stirring.
4. Serve warm or cold with half and half cream.

▤Baked Apples

4	4	large apples
50 mL	¼	cup melted butter or margarine
25 mL	4	heaping teaspoons brown sugar
2 mL	½	teaspoon cinnamon
50 mL	¼	cup precooked raisins
25 mL	4	teaspoons chopped walnuts

1. Core apples and peel a strip from top of each apple.
2. Place apples in an 8″ (20 cm) round microproof baking dish.
3. Melt butter or margarine in a 1 cup (250 mL) measuring pitcher.
4. Stir sugar, cinnamon, raisins and walnuts. Fill each apple with mixture.
5. Cover with plastic wrap and microwave 5 minutes on *high*.
6. Standing time 5 minutes.

▤Old Fashioned Pineapple Upside Down Cake

50 mL	¼	cup butter or margarine
125 mL	½	cup brown sugar
398 mL	14	oz can pineapple slices (drained) save the juice maraschino cherries
255 g	9	oz package white or yellow cake mix

1. Melt butter in an 8″ (20 cm) or 9″ (23 cm) round cake pan, for 30 seconds on *high*.
2. Stir in brown sugar. Place pineapple slices on top of brown sugar and butter or margarine. Place cherries in centres of pineapple slices.
3. Prepare cake mix according to package directions, substituting pineapple juice for water.
4. Spoon half of the cake batter over the pineapple.
5. Microwave 8-9 minutes on *medium high*.
6. Let baked cake stand 2-4 minutes. Invert onto a cake plate.

Extra Tips for Remaining Cake Batter

1. Use cake batter for cup cakes; makes 4-5 cup cakes. Microwave 2 minutes on *medium high*.
2. Fill flat based ice cream cones ⅓ full. Microwave 2 minutes on *medium high*. Frost cupcakes or ice cream cups with favorite icing.

 Re-heating Pastry — Sugary buns, such as donuts, bismarks, cinnamon buns, and all kinds of pastry, heat from the inside out. Care must be taken not to heat too long. 10-15 seconds on high for one is sufficient.

▤Golden Carrot Cake

2	2	eggs
125 mL	½	cup cooking oil
187 mL	¾	cup brown sugar
250 mL	1	cup finely grated carrots
187 mL	¾	cup flour (whole wheat)
5 mL	1	teaspoon baking powder
2 mL	½	teaspoon soda
5 mL	1	teaspoon cinnamon
1 mL	¼	teaspoon nutmeg
50 mL	¼	cup finely chopped nuts

1. Beat together the eggs, cooking oil, brown sugar, and grated carrots on low speed.
2. Add the remaining ingredients and beat at medium speed for 2 minutes.
3. Grease one round 8″ (20 cm) layer cake plate or line bottom of cake plate with wax paper for easier removal.
4. Microwave cake on *medium* for 6 minutes. Increase power to *medium high*. Microwave 6-8 minutes. Cool and frost with cream cheese frosting. Repeat recipe for second layer if required.

Cream Cheese Frosting

30 mL	2	Tablespoons butter or margarine
125 g	4	oz cream cheese
15 mL	1	Tablespoon cream or ½ and ½ cream
625 mL	2½-3	cups icing sugar

1. In a mixing bowl combine butter, cream cheese and cream
2. Microwave on *medium* for 30 seconds until warm
3. Mix well and beat in icing sugar until spreadable. If too thick, add a few drops of cream.
For one layer, use half the cream cheese frosting.
4. Microwave cake on *medium* for 6 minutes. Increase power to *high*. Microwave 2-3 minutes. Cool and frost with cream cheese frosting. Repeat recipe for second layer if required.

▤Lemony Cheese Pie

Graham Cracker Crust

416 mL	1⅔	cups graham cracker crumbs
125 mL	½	cup butter or margarine
50 mL	¼	cup sugar
1 mL	¼	teaspoon cinnamon (optional)

1. Melt butter or margarine in a round 9″ (23 cm) glass pie plate; 30 seconds on *high*.
2. Add crumbs, sugar and cinnamon, mix well, press against bottom and sides of pie plate.
3. Microwave 2 minutes on *medium high*.

Filling

250 g	8	oz cream cheese
125 mL	½	cup lemon juice
2	2	eggs, beaten
125 mL	½	cup sugar
250 mL	1	cup sour cream
5 mL	1	teaspoon grated lemon rind (or dried lemon rind)
15 mL	1	Tablespoon sugar

1. Soften cream cheese 30 seconds on *medium high*.
2. In a mixing bowl beat cream cheese and lemon juice until smooth.
3. Add beaten eggs and sugar, beat until fluffy.
4. Pour into graham cracker crust.
5. Microwave 5-6 minutes on *medium high* until filling is set.
6. Combine sour cream, lemon rind and sugar, spread over filling. Microwave 2 minutes on *medium high*.

Variation

1. Spoon cherry or blueberry pie filling on top of cheese cake.

≡Apple Graham Pie

125 mL	½	cup butter or margarine
50 mL	¼	cup sugar
500 mL	2	cups graham wafer crumbs
1250 mL	5	cups thinly sliced apples (4-6 medium)
125 mL	½	cup sugar
5 mL	1	teaspoon cinnamon

1. Melt butter or margarine in a round 9″ (23 cm) glass pie plate, 30 seconds on *high*.
2. Add sugar, and crumbs. Mix well and press against bottom and sides of pie plate. Save some crumbs for topping.
3. In mixing bowl combine apple slices, sugar and cinnamon, mixing well.
4. Place apples into graham crust and top with remaining crumbs.
5. Microwave 10-12 minutes on *medium high* or until apples are soft.
6. Serve warm or cold.

 Softening Brown Sugar — Put a wedge of apple, or a damp paper towel in a shallow microproof dish with the brown sugar. Cover and microwave 2-3 minutes on *medium* or until soft.

▤Grasshopper Pie

1	1	box of plain chocolate cookies
1	1	package large marshmallows
125 mL	½	cup milk
30 mL	2	Tablespoons green crème de menthe
30 mL	2	Tablespoons of crème de cacao
4-5	4-5	drops green food coloring (optional)
250 mL	1	cup whipping cream

1. Place round chocolate cookies on bottom and sides of a round 9″ (23 cm) pie plate.
2. Combine marshmallows and milk in a large glass mixing bowl. Microwave on *high* for 2-3 minutes or until marshmallows start to puff. Stir to blend.
3. Stir in liqueurs with food coloring. Mix well.
4. Cool 30-40 minutes until slightly thickened, stirring occasionally.
5. Fold whipped cream into mixture and pour over chocolate cookies. Refrigerate for at least 4 hours.
6. Garnish with more whipped cream and chocolate curls.

Variations

Brandy Alexander Pie
Stir 2 Tablespoons (30 mL) of crème de cacao and 2 Tablespoons (30 mL) of brandy in blended marshmallows. Mix well.

Kahlua Pie
Add 1 teaspoon (5 mL) instant coffee powder to blended marshmallows and 2 Tablespoons (30 mL) Kahlua. Mix well.

Amaretto Pie
Add ¼ cup (50 mL) Amaretto into blended marshmallows. Mix well.

▤Flaming Cherries Jubilee

796 mL	2-	14 oz cans dark sweet cherries (drained), reserve juice
50 mL	3	Tablespoons cornstarch
15 mL	1	Tablespoon lemon juice
5 mL	1	teaspoon grated lemon rind
125 mL	½	cup sugar
125 mL	½	cup brandy

1. In a 2 quart (2L) casserole dish mix cherry juice, cornstarch, lemon juice, grated lemon rind and sugar. Stir well.
2. Microwave 4-5 minutes on *high*, stirring mixture twice until sauce thickens.
3. Add cherries, stirring well.
4. Microwave brandy in a 1 cup (250 mL) measuring pitcher, 20 seconds on *high* until hot.
5. Pour 1 Tablespoon (15 mL) heated brandy into metal spoon and remaining brandy over top of cherries. Ignite brandy on spoon and pour over brandy and cherries.
6. This flame looks very effective when lights are low.
7. Serve on ice cream when flame has subsided.

A Baked-look Appearance — To give quick breads or white cakes a baked-look appearance, grease baking dish lightly, and sprinkle with either of the following crumbs: wheat germ, crushed graham or vanilla cookies or cornflake crumbs. These will stick to the pan. Pour batter in and cook cake.

▤ Easy Peanut Butter Slice

250 mL	1	cup butter or margarine
250 mL	1	cup peanut butter
500 mL	2	cups graham cracker crumbs
125 mL	½	cup finely chopped walnuts or peanuts
500 mL	2	cups icing sugar or more
250 mL	1	cup chocolate chipits or dipping chocolate
30 mL	2	Tablespoons butter or margarine

1. Combine butter or margarine and peanut butter in a medium glass mixing bowl.
2. Microwave 1-2 minutes on *high*, until melted. Stir well.
3. Mix in crumbs, nuts and sugar, until mixture is stiff. Press firmly into a lightly buttered 9″ x 9″ (2.5L) cake baking dish.
4. In a small bowl combine chocolate chipits and butter or margarine. Microwave 2 minutes on *medium*. Mix well and spread on top of peanut butter slice.
5. Cool and slice.

▤ Peanut Butter Marshmallow Bars

125 mL	½	cup butter or margarine
250 mL	1	cup peanut butter
350 g	1	large package butterscotch chipits
350 g	1	large package chocolate chipits
1	1	package of colored miniature marshmallows
187 mL	¾	cup coconut (fine flake)
125 mL	½	cup chopped walnuts

1. Melt butter or margarine, peanut butter and chips, together in a 2 quart (2L) microproof measuring pitcher, for 2-4 minutes on *medium*. Stir twice to blend ingredients.
2. Cool slightly, add marshmallows, coconuts and walnuts.
3. Press lightly into a 9″ x 9″ (2.5L) cake pan.
4. Cool and slice.

≡Mincemeat Crumb Squares

166 mL	⅔	cup brown sugar
1 mL	¼	teaspoon salt
250 mL	1	cup quick cooking rolled oats
250 mL	1	cup flour
125 mL	½	cup butter or margarine
250 mL	1	cup mincemeat

1. Mix brown sugar, salt, rolled oats and flour into a mixing bowl.
2. Cut butter or margarine into the dry ingredients until crumbly.
3. Press crumbs, except for 1 cup, into an 8″ x 8″ (2L) microproof baking dish.
4. Microwave crumb base for 3-5 minutes on *medium*, or just until partly done.
5. Spread mincemeat on crumb base and sprinkle 1 cup (250 mL) crumb mixture on top.
6. Microwave on *medium high* for 6-8 minutes.
7. Use whip cream or ice cream for topping.

Extra Tip

Date filling can be used instead of mincemeat

250 mL	1	cup dates, chopped
83 mL	⅓	cup water
50 mL	3	Tablespoons sugar
15 mL	1	Tablespoon lemon juice

1. Combine chopped dates, water, sugar and lemon juice in a mixing bowl.
2. Microwave on *medium high* 3-5 minutes until thick and spreadable.
3. Stir date mixture every minute, as this mixture burns rapidly.

Jiffy Strawberry Shortcake

255 g	9	oz package white or yellow cake mix (one layer)
250 mL	½	pint whipping cream (whipped)
		Fresh or frozen strawberries

1. Prepare cake mix according to package directions.
2. Grease an 8″ x 8″ (2L) microproof baking dish. Pour cake batter into baking dish spreading evenly.
3. Place foil shiny side up on corners of cake pan. Microwave 5 minutes on *medium high*.
4. Remove foil and microwave 3 minutes on *high*.
5. Cool cake, cut into squares.
6. Serve with whipped cream and strawberries on top.
7. Nice for a quick summer dessert.

Sour Cream Raisin Nut Slice

2	2	eggs
125 mL	½	cup brown sugar
50 mL	¼	cup butter or margarine
5 mL	1	teaspoon vanilla
125 mL	½	cup sour cream
125 mL	½	cup raisins, partly cooked
250 mL	1	cup flour
2 mL	½	teaspoon soda
1 mL	¼	teaspoon salt
50 mL	¼	cup chopped nuts

1. In a medium mixing bowl, mix eggs, brown sugar, butter or margarine, vanilla and sour cream.
2. Add raisins, which have been microwaved on *medium high*, for 2 minutes. Cook raisins with ¼ cup (50 mL) water. Drain raisins well.
3. Add flour, soda, salt and chopped nuts to liquid mixture.
4. Mix well and spread into greased 9″ x 9″ (2.5L) microproof baking dish.
5. Place foil shiny side up on four corners of baking dish. Microwave 5 minutes on *medium high*. Remove foil and microwave 3-4 minutes on *high*.
6. Use your favorite frosting. Spread evenly on warm slice.

≡Chocolate Chow Mein Noodle Clusters

| 170 g | 6 | oz package semi-sweet chocolate chips |
| 84 g | 3 | oz can chow mein noodles |

1. Microwave chocolate chips in a 3 quart (3L) microproof mixing bowl for 2-4 minutes on *medium*.
2. Stir chocolate until smooth. Add noodles and using 2 forks, toss to coat well.
3. Form into teaspoonful clusters, on wax paper.
4. Cool to set.

≡Chocolate Raisin Nut Clusters

250 mL	1	cup seedless raisins
170 g	6	oz package chocolate chips
250 mL	1	cup peanuts

1. Place all ingredients in a 2 quart (2L) microproof casserole dish.
2. Microwave 2-4 minutes on *medium* or until chocolate is melted.
3. Stir mixture while chocolate is melting.
4. Stir mixture until chocolate coats peanuts and raisins.
5. Drop by teaspoonful onto wax paper. Chill until firm.

Melting Chocolate — For recipes which require melted chocolate; place chocolate chips or broken pieces in a microproof dish and microwave for 2-4 minutes on *medium*. Stir twice, as chocolate holds its shape.

≣Chocolate Covered Amaretto Balls

125 mL	½	cup butter or margarine, melted
500 mL	2	cups fine vanilla wafer crumbs
125 mL	½	cup finely chopped nuts
50 mL	¼	cup amaretto liqueur
6	6	squares semi-sweet chocolate

1. Melt butter or margarine for 30 seconds on *high*, in a microproof bowl.
2. Mix all ingredients except chocolate. Stir together. Shape mixture into 1″ (2.5 cm) balls. Refrigerate for ½-1 hour.
3. In a 1 quart (1L) microproof bowl, melt chocolate squares for 2-4 minutes on *medium*. Stir at least twice.
4. Dip balls into chocolate; coating well. Place on wax paper lined cookie sheet and refrigerate until set.

≣Peanut Brittle

250 mL	1	cup sugar
125 mL	½	cup white corn syrup
250 mL	1	cup roasted, salted peanuts
5 mL	1	teaspoon butter or margarine
5 mL	1	teaspoon vanilla
5 mL	1	teaspoon baking soda

1. Microwave sugar and corn syrup in a 2 quart (2L) microproof measuring pitcher, on *high* for 4 minutes. Stir once at 2 minutes.
2. Stir in peanuts, microwave 3-5 minutes on *high*, until light brown.
3. Add butter or margarine and vanilla to syrup, stirring well. Microwave 1-2 minutes on *high*. This mixture is extremely hot.
4. Add baking soda and stir until light and foamy.
5. Pour mixture onto greased cookie sheet. Let cool ½-1 hour. Break into small pieces and store in air tight container.

Extra Tip

Almonds, pecans or cashew nuts can be used instead of peanuts.

≣Mocha Truffles

170 g	6	oz package semi-sweet chocolate chips
83 mL	⅓	cup butter or margarine
10 mL	2	teaspoons instant coffee powder
50 mL	3	Tablespoons coffee liqueur
1	1	egg yolk
250 mL	1	cup sifted icing sugar
166 mL	⅔	cup dark chocolate sprinkles

1. Place chocolate, butter or margarine and coffee powder, in a micro-proof 2 quart (2L) measuring pitcher.
2. Microwave for 2-4 minutes on *medium*.
3. Let mixture cool 5 minutes.
4. Stir in 2 Tablespoons (30 mL) liqueur and egg yolk.
5. Slowly blend in icing sugar. Chill for ½-1 hour or until cool to handle.
6. Roll into 1″ (2.5 cm) balls. Dip balls into remaining 1 Tablespoon (15 mL) liqueur and into chocolate sprinkles. Store in air tight container in fridge.

≣Fresh Apple or Peach Crisp

1500 mL	6	cups cooking apples or peaches
125 mL	½	cup whole wheat flour
125 mL	½	cup rolled oats
187 mL	¾	cup brown sugar
5 mL	1	teaspoon cinnamon
1 mL	¼	teaspoon nutmeg
50-125 mL	¼-½	cup butter or margarine

1. Place sliced apples or peaches in a 8″ x 8″ (2L) glass baking dish.
2. Combine remaining ingredients in mixing bowl and cut in butter, until crumbly.
3. Sprinkle crumb mixture on apples or peaches
4. Sprinkle cinnamon on top of mixture, for added color.
5. Use foil, shiny side up, on corners of square baking dish. Microwave 6 minutes on *high*.
6. Remove foil and continue to microwave 8-10 minutes on *high*, until apples or peaches are soft.
7. Standing time 5 minutes.

▤Chocolate Honey Squares

83 mL	⅓	cup butter or margarine
125 mL	½	cup cocoa
83 mL	⅓	cup honey
750 mL	3	cups miniature marshmallows
5 mL	1	teaspoon vanilla
1L	4	cups rice krispies
250 mL	1	cup nuts (optional)

1. Melt butter or margarine in a 2 quart (2L) microproof measuring pitcher for 30 seconds on *high*.
2. Blend cocoa and honey into butter.
3. Add marshmallows and microwave for 2 minutes on *high*.
4. Add vanilla and stir mixture well.
5. Add rice krispies and peanuts.
6. Press lightly into a greased 9" x 9" (2.5L) cake pan.
7. Cool, cut into squares.

▤Rice Krispies Mallow Bars

125 mL	½	cup butter or margarine
50 mL	¼	cup peanut butter
1	1	package miniature marshmallows
1250 mL	5	cups rice krispies
500 mL	2	cups salted peanuts (optional)

Topping

250 mL	1	cup chocolate chips
50 mL	¼	cup peanut butter

1. Microwave butter or margarine and peanut butter, in a 2 quart (2L) microwave proof measuring pitcher, for 1 minute on *high* or until melted.
2. Stir in marshmallows, microwave for 2 minutes on *high*, until melted, stirring every minute. Stir until smooth.
3. Add cereal and peanuts, mix until cereal is coated.
4. Press mixture into a buttered 9" x 9" (2.5L) baking dish with a large spoon, dipped in cold water or lightly buttered, to prevent sticking.
5. Melt topping in a small glass bowl, for 2 minutes on *medium*. Mix well and spread over bars. Cool before cutting.

≣Seven Layer Bars

125 mL	½	cup butter or margarine
375 mL	1½	cups graham cracker crumbs
250 mL	1	cup chopped walnuts
250 mL	1	cup semi-sweet chocolate chips
250 mL	1	cup butterscotch chips
250 mL	1	cup flaked coconut
300 mL	14	oz can sweetened condensed milk

1. In a microproof 9″ x 9″ (2.5L) baking dish, microwave butter or margarine for 30 seconds on *high*.
2. Add graham cracker crumbs and mix thoroughly. Press firmly into baking dish. Alternating layers, add walnuts, chocolate chips, butterscotch chips, coconut and top with condensed milk.
3. Place foil, shiny side up on four corners of baking dish. Microwave 5 minutes on *medium high*. Remove foil and continue to microwave 5 minutes on *medium high*.
4. Cool and slice.

Extra Tip

Chopped green and red cherries can be added for the festive season.

 Toasting Coconut — Sprinkle 1 cup (250 mL) flaked coconut in a microproof pie plate. Microwave 2-3 minutes on *high*, uncovered. Stir at 2 minutes.

☰Microwave Brownies

2	2	squares of chocolate or ½ cup (125 mL) cocoa
125 mL	½	cup butter or margarine
250 mL	1	cup sugar
2	2	eggs
250 mL	1	cup unsifted flour
1 mL	¼	teaspoon baking powder
1 mL	¼	teaspoon salt
2 mL	½	teaspoon vanilla
125 mL	½	cup chopped walnuts

1. Mix chocolate squares or cocoa and butter or margarine in a medium sized mixing bowl.
2. Microwave on *medium high* for 1-1½ minutes, until butter and chocolate are melted.
3. Add sugar and eggs, stirring well.
4. Add flour, baking powder, salt, vanilla and chopped walnuts. Mix well.
5. Spread into a lightly greased 9″ x 9″ (2.5L) microproof baking dish.
6. Place foil, shiny side up on four corners of baking dish. Microwave for 5 minutes on *medium high*. Remove foil, then microwave 3-4 minutes on *high*.
7. Cool until set then cut into bars.

Extra Tip

Place colored miniature marshmallows evenly on top of brownies. Microwave 1-2 minutes on *high*. Marshmallows will stick together. Cool well and frost with chocolate icing.

☰Strawberry or Raspberry Sauce

283 mL	10	oz package sweetened berries, thawed
10 mL	2	teaspoons cornstarch or tapioca starch
15 mL	1	Tablespoon lemon juice
3	3	drops red food color (optional)

1. Combine cornstarch, lemon juice and berry juice in a 4 cup (1L) measuring cup.
2. Stir in berries and microwave 2-4 minutes on *high* uncovered, or until thickened. Stir twice.
3. Stir in food color. Serve warm or cold on your favorite dessert.
4. Serves 8-10.

☰Lemon Sauce

50 mL	¼	cup butter or margarine
250 mL	1	cup sugar
15 mL	1	Tablespoon cornstarch
83 mL	⅓	cup water
83 mL	⅓	cup lemon juice
15 mL	1	Tablespoon grated lemon peel
2	2	eggs, beaten

1. Cream butter or margarine, sugar and cornstarch in a 4 cup (1L) measuring pitcher.
2. Stir in water, lemon juice, lemon peel and beaten eggs.
3. Microwave 4-6 minutes on *medium* uncovered, stirring twice.
4. Serve warm on favorite desserts.
5. Serves 6-8.

≣Hot Fudge Sauce

250 mL	1	cup semi-sweet chocolate chips
15 mL	1	Tablespoon butter or margarine
125 mL	½	cup light corn syrup
50 mL	¼	cup half and half cream, or whipping cream
5 mL	1	teaspoon vanilla flavoring

1. Combine chocolate chips, butter or margarine and corn syrup in a 4 cup (1L) measuring pitcher.
2. Microwave 3-4 minutes on *medium* uncovered.
3. Stir once, gradually adding half and half cream and vanilla. Stir until smooth.
4. Microwave 1 minute on *medium*.

Extra Tip

For a different flavor add 1 teaspoon (5 mL) rum extract or ½ teaspoon (2 mL) mint extract instead of vanilla.

≣Blueberry Sauce

398 mL	14	oz can blueberry fruit
50 mL	¼	cup sugar
15 mL	1	Tablespoon lemon juice
30 mL	2	Tablespoons cornstarch or tapioca starch

1. In a 4 cup (1L) measuring pitcher mix undrained blueberry fruit, sugar and lemon juice.
2. Stir cornstarch or tapioca starch into mixture.
3. Microwave 4 minutes on *high* uncovered. Stir. Microwave 2 minutes on *high*, or until sauce is thickened and clear.
4. Serve over pancakes, waffles, and ice cream.
5. Makes 1½ cups (375 mL).

▤Index

135

Juss Microwaving

Name

Address ···

City ···

Province/State ························ Postal Code/Zip ·········

Please send ················· copies of
JUSS MICROWAVING at $8.95 per copy plus $1.50 for
postage and handling

Cheque or money order enclosed for ············
Payable to: JUSS MICROWAVING PUBLISHING CO.
P.O. Box 762
Medicine Hat, Alberta
T1A 7G7 Canada

Juss Microwaving

Name ···

Address ···

City ···

Province/State ······················ Postal Code/Zip ·········

Please send ················· copies of
JUSS MICROWAVING at $8.95 per copy plus $1.50 for
postage and handling

Cheque or money order enclosed for ············
Payable to: JUSS MICROWAVING PUBLISHING CO.
P.O. Box 762
Medicine Hat, Alberta
T1A 7G7 Canada